YOU
THE MAIL ON SUNDAY
M A G A Z I N E

BOOK OF
JOURNOLISTS

JOHN KOSKI is Associate Editor of YOU Magazine. These days he finds it difficult to write a shopping list.

MITCHELL SYMONS is a former BBC TV director who writes for a variety of publications, including a regular column in *Punch*. As well as writing lists, he devises television game shows and compiles fiendishly difficult crosswords.

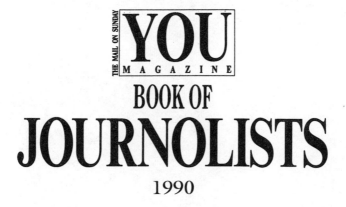

BOOK OF
JOURNOLISTS
1990

John Koski and Mitchell Symons

Cartoons by Ian Dicks

Chapmans
1990

Chapmans Publishers Ltd
141–143 Drury Lane
London WC2B 5TB

BRITISH LIBRARY CATALOGUING IN PUBLICATION DATA
The You magazine book of journolists . . .
1990 –
1. Miscellaneous facts
I. You magazine
032.02

ISBN 1–85592–705–5

First published by Chapmans 1990

Photoset in 11/13 Galliard by
Ace Filmsetting Ltd, Frome, Somerset
Printed and bound in Great Britain by
Clays Ltd, St Ives plc

ACKNOWLEDGEMENTS

Welcome to the second YOU Magazine *Book of Journolists*. Once again, we must thank all our readers, who continue to provide encouragement and inspiration by sending in their own ideas for lists.

Many thanks to Sara Driver for her invaluable research.

And extra-special thanks to our four most prolific and inventive contributors: Malcolm Burgess, Donnie Kerr, Steve Clothier and Mike Barwell.

The Way We Live Now

Are you middle-class? Ten tell-tale signs

Apologising for not offering real coffee
Not wearing make-up in Sainsbury's
Moving house to be near a good school
Reading the ingredients on food packets
Forcing your children to attend piano lessons

Buying Christmas presents from Oxfam
Organising a neighbourhood watch
Buying books even when you're not going on holiday
Throwing parties at Sunday lunchtime
Going for weekend breaks at country house hotels

The honeymoon period is over when . . .

He notices a new dress only when it appears on the Access bill
The dog fetches the slippers and she does the barking
They take turns in the shower
He opens his mouth only to yawn
They begin calling each other by their proper names
She explains how the washing machine works
They buy a TV for the bedroom
He asks whatever happened to his football scarf
She buys him a power drill for his birthday
He asks for a power drill for his birthday

Know your car: those technical terms explained

Shock absorber: Padded leather chair at BMW dealer
Automatic choke: Involuntary reaction to repair bills

Cylinder bore: Vintage car enthusiast
Spoiler: Radar trap
In-car entertainment: Equipment fitted for the amusement of
    garage servicing staff
Tune: Something which helps your engine breathe more
    easily
Stability control: Police car parked outside the pub
Cooling system: Windows
Power steering: Chauffeur
Fuel injection: Something that hurts your wallet

Ten modern laws

People who eat natural foods die of natural causes
A politician will always be there when he needs you
If everyone else has a flu vaccination, you don't need one
If it wasn't for the last minute, nothing would get done
Beware of buying anything when the manuals are bigger than
    the equipment
You never want the one you can afford
Never play cat-and-mouse games if you're a mouse
Inflation allows you to live in a more expensive
    neighbourhood without moving
Your favourite song comes on the car radio when you reach
    your destination
Good judgement comes from experience, and experience
    comes from bad judgement

Are you suffering the mid-life crisis? Ten tell-tale signs

You're seriously thinking of buying underwear from Next
    instead of M&S
You're worried that your wife might start shoplifting
Crofting in Scotland seems a viable alternative
You've faced up to it: flares are never coming back
The classic 'Bobby Charlton' doesn't seem like a bad hairstyle
    after all
Reading job ads sends you into a deep depression
Nose-hair trimmers don't seem funny any more
You think buying a sports car might cheer you up
You're worried that women might find you a bit boring
Women find you boring

Shame on you! Ten things you really shouldn't do

Say 'I've already given' when a charity collector asks for a donation

Feel annoyed with people who fall on the line during rush hour

Examine the contents of other people's bathroom cabinets

Wear last year's Remembrance Day poppy

Empty your car ashtrays in someone else's street

Go into a bookshop to look something up in the *Good Food Guide*

Hope that Richard Branson's balloon gets a puncture

Tell your children they're too old for the tooth fairy

Open presents carefully so you can save the wrapping paper

Insist that you thought the Little Chef bill included service

The greasy pole – where do you stand?

Chairman: Someone who has never heard the word 'No'

Director: A man whose letters are signed in his absence

Non-executive Director: Willing to do an honest day's work for a full month's pay

Executive: A big gun who has succeeded in not being fired

Accountant: A man who comes to a different conclusion when he adds up your expenses

Manager: Person who takes responsibility when things go right

Trainee: Too young to have bad habits, but is willing to learn

Secretary: Good at filing, especially nails

Messenger: Someone who thinks it is better to receive than to give

Tea lady: A woman who thinks money grows on trays

Are you a failure? Ten tell-tale signs

Your boss is younger than you
You think the prizes on TV game shows are worth having
You've never owned a car which didn't need an MoT
    certificate
You don't give to Oxfam shops, you buy from them
You're over thirty and still travel by bus
Your second home is a caravan
You've never received junk mail from American Express
Nobody is remotely jealous of you
You don't know enough people to throw a party
You've never moved house

Ten things you intend to do when you're older

Learn to play bridge
Grow your own vegetables
Take the advanced driving test
Write a book
Apply to become a magistrate
Do charity work
Go back to university
Change your career
Read something by Dostoevsky
Learn to relax

The ten laws of queueing

Queues exist only when you join them
Queue size is inversely proportional to the waiting time
     available
Your queue starts to move only when you leave it to join
     another one
Queues form behind you only when you're buying something
     embarrassing at the chemist's
The number of counters open is the square root of your
     expected parking fine
If bank queues move quickly, it means you've forgotten your
     cheque book
At the express checkout the person in front counts ten
     yoghurts as one item
In fast food restaurants you're always behind the world's
     largest family
Counter staff have the same lunch hours as you
Just when you think you're home and dry, the checkout girl
     finds an item without a price on it

Entertainer-speak: a guide to interpretation

Thank you for being a wonderful audience: Thank you for
    turning up

This song means a lot to me: It was my only hit

Feel free to clap along with this one: Let me know there's
    someone out there

Northern audiences are the best in the world: Unless I'm in
    London, when Southern audiences are the best in the
    world

And now a song one or two of you might know: Yes, it's *My
    Way*

Any Liverpool supporters here tonight?: I'll do anything to
    get a cheer

If I offend anyone, it's only in good fun: I tell racist and sexist
    jokes

And here's one for all you ladies out there: That's right, it's
    Feelings

This reminds me of when I played Caesar's Palace: Caesar's
    Palace, Luton

But seriously, folks . . . : In case you missed it, that was a joke

A guide to the North-South divide

In the North . . .

People go to work in the next street

Everyone thinks Birmingham is in the South

You get change from a £5 note in a pub

People think the North is hard done by

They're having the last laugh over house prices

Ice creams cost less than £1

Tory MPs are an endangered species

Hurricanes rate a few lines on page five

They think *EastEnders* is real life

Shop assistants call you 'luv'

In the South . . .

People go to work in the next county

Everyone thinks Birmingham is in the North

It costs £5 to get into a pub

People think Northerners don't know when they're well-off

One more mortgage increase and everybody's off to Yorkshire

Only tourists buy ice creams

Tory MPs are about to become an endangered species

Anything above a stiff breeze makes the *Nine O'Clock News*

They think *thirtysomething* is real life

Shop assistants ignore you

Small business-speak: a guide to interpretation

Networking: Lunch at the Rotary Club
Business centre: Photocopier in the spare bedroom
Re-financing package: Second mortgage
Marketing: Handing out business cards
Associates: Wife
Capital investment: Headed writing paper
Market-led: T-shirt concession for the lambada
1992: Who knows, something might turn up
Advertising campaign: Entry in *Yellow Pages*
Independent: Overdraft facility withdrawn

Those weekend breaks: a guide to interpretation

Shakespeare Country: Traffic jams outside Stratford-on-Avon
Howard's Way Country: Marina and nautical boutique on the
    Solent
Hardy's Wessex: Could be anywhere in the South of England
Constable Country: Packed tea-rooms in North Essex
Gainsborough Country: Packed tea-rooms in South Suffolk
Robin Hood Country: Nottingham outer ring road
Hereward Country: Flat bits near Cambridge
Herriot Country: Most of Yorkshire
Lowry Country: Redeveloped docks in Salford
Cookson Country: Gateshead Metro Centre

Post-everything: a guide to interpretation

Post-industrial: Nation of shops selling nothing but
     earthenware pomanders
Post-funk: Kylie and Jason
Post-style: Sofas which are comfortable
Post-modernism: Yes, we have no bananas
Post-structuralism: Nobody knows what this means
Post-Marxist: East Europeans going on package holidays
Post-AIDS: Celibacy can be fun
Post-Thatcherism: Nobody knows what this means, either
Post-1992: 1993
Post-prandial: Drunk

Life's too short to . . .

Read another profile of Kenneth Branagh
Make your own mayonnaise
Play board games with people who can't stand losing
Explain the rules of cricket to an American
Attend a timeshare presentation
Use the whitener you bought for your tennis shoes
Open junk mail
Peel a grape
Read the operating manual for a new car
Wait for Esperanto to become the world language

Ten things men do that irritate women

Leave the toilet seat up
Suggest that a woman at home all day has nothing to do
Leave dirty socks inside out
Claim total inability to work the washing machine
Forget to cut their toenails
Throw wet towels on the bed
Compliment other women on their clothes
Leave used sports gear in the car boot for weeks
Buy presents of totally impractical underwear
Feel insecure if a woman earns more than they do

Ten things women do that irritate men

Stuff the car ashtrays with Kleenex
Keep your embarrassing love letters
Point out the streaks on the glasses you've washed up
Try to make you eat healthier food
Read magazine articles which suggest your libido is seriously
    below average
Treat plants like children
Want to get engaged
Say 'Don't you think you've had enough to drink?'
Drag you to the sales
Wonder why you need to go to the pub when there's plenty
    of beer in the fridge

Divided by a common language – interpreting how Americans see us

English rose: Joan Collins
Folk custom: Walking
Dickensian: Pub toilets
Cute: Policemen without guns
British sense of humour: Laughing at *Dynasty*
Ancient tradition: Queueing
Neighbours: London and Edinburgh
Historical: Warm beer
Culture: *Starlight Express*
Typical locals: Morris dancers

Ten reasons to welcome the Greenhouse Effect

Your home is getting closer to the seaside
It makes a change from worrying about AIDS
You can get to know your neighbours better at the street
     standpipe
Belgium will disappear
Ski-ing bores will have nothing to talk about
It's about time Nicholas Lyndhurst got some colour in his
     cheeks
No more waiting around at airports for summer holidays
Lower fuel bills
Soccer managers will give up wearing sheepskin coats
You can get rid of your greenhouse

Get fit with the workaholics' work-out routine

Keep your nose to the grindstone
Put your shoulder to the wheel
Keep your eye on the ball
Keep your ear to the ground
Work your fingers to the bone
Put your best foot forward
Keep your head down
Keep your hand in
Put your back into it
Keep your hair on

Ten ways to keep warm this winter

Burn your British Gas share certificates
Burrow underneath the junk mail stuffed through your door
Camp outside an estate agent who sells holiday cottages in
     Wales
Line your clothing with Caribbean holiday brochures
Put Mates on all your fingers and toes
Go bathing near a nuclear power station
Convert *The Sunday Times* into handy fire bricks
Have an indoor barbecue
Discard the remote control and get up to switch channels
Create your own greenhouse effect – move into the
     greenhouse

Feel like getting away from it all? Ten safe places to hide

The House of Commons on a Friday afternoon
Wimbledon FC's midfield
Satellite Television (on screen)
A Gyles Brandreth book signing
In a revival of *Ziegfeld*
At a midweek county cricket match
An Abbey National shareholders' meeting
Wherever Shergar is
At a symposium on the works of Salman Rushdie
In Yorkshire County Cricket Club's trophy room

Leaving card-speak: a guide to interpretation

You'll be missed: You're not being replaced
All the best: I'm too busy to think of anything witty to say
Office parties won't be the same: The photocopier still
    doesn't work properly
Come back and see us: Come back and gloat
Keep in touch: Because we won't
Hope your teeth are better now: You certainly had enough
    'dental appointments' while you were here
I've enjoyed working with you: We met once in the lift
You deserve it: You always were pushy
I'll watch your career with interest: And hope you don't do
    too well
Best of luck!: Whoever you are

Ten things that should be made illegal

Plastic cutlery
Car horns which play *Colonel Bogey*
Arriving late at the theatre
Tipping taxi drivers
'Funny' car stickers
Telephone muzak while you hang on
Car alarms which go off if you breathe within twenty yards of
them
Street theatre
Eating hamburgers on the Tube
Freezer bags you can't open

Ten things they'll make illegal one day

Leaving your car door unlocked
Standing two abreast on escalators
Smoking in a built-up area
Being overweight
Walking the wrong way down a one-way street
Cash
Booking at a restaurant and not showing up
Travelling in a car without a crash helmet
Not using the postcode
Swatting flies

The ten laws of office life

Length of lunch break is directly proportional to size of salary

Work expands to fill the time until the pubs open

The fridge always smells like a biology lab

Waiting time for the lift is exactly double the time it would take to use the stairs

The more functions a photocopier has, the more often it breaks down

Temporary secretaries leave the day after you finally remember their names

However early you get in, someone else is already there

The boss's jokes are always the funniest

Too much coffee can keep you awake in the afternoons

There is never any water in the kettle

'But I know a man who can't' – ten things the AA man won't come out for

The nodding dog's head won't nod
The ashtrays are full
The furry dice are tangled
You've run out of travel sweets
The radio only picks up Hilversum
You can't re-fold your road map of Great Britain
Garfield keeps falling off
You can't pay the Little Chef bill
The kids have spilt orange juice on the back seat
The glove compartment is full of fluffy Polo mints

Ten things to look forward to in the next Budget

An increase in the married man's lager allowance
VAT on beards
Full charitable status for off-licences
An increase in the child allowance for couples over the age of
    eighty
Poll Tax subsidy for Conservative constituencies
No increase in the Road Fund licence, except for Porsche
    owners
Introduction of a dandruff tax
A reduction in standard tacks
VAT on sticky buns
Privatisation of the Inland Revenue

Ten things which don't seem to exist

Proper Coke bottles
Complete programmes of *The Two Ronnies*
Anyone to answer the phone at West End theatres
Wine bars which don't play the Gypsy Kings
Batteries in packs of one
Butchers who read the same recipes as you do
Dry cleaners who don't mangle silk ties
Signs saying 'Feel free to smoke'
Food which is safe to eat
Good news

That InterCity experience – ten things the BR ads don't show

Lager cans rolling around the aisles
People standing
Mountains of orange peel on the tables
People trying the door when you're in the loo
The long march to the buffet
Juggling with your drink on the way back
Scalding your fingers every time the train jolts
Plastic cups with cigarette burns in them
Fractious children
Staff shortages

Adspeak: a guide to interpretation

Tests prove . . . . : Anything we want, since we paid for them
Comes in regular or economy size: Comes in small or
     medium
Contains full-cream milk: So what?
New formula: New packaging
Winter sale ends this week!: Spring sale starts next week
Eats up the miles: Eats up the petrol
Now better than ever: Sorry the last lot didn't work
Pays for itself: All you have to do is sign the cheque
Fully guaranteed: To break down when the guarantee runs
     out
Save £££s!: Spend £££s

Ten places to spot a parked Ford Escort RS Turbo

In a hedge
On the hard shoulder in front of a police car
On the pavement by a bank cash machine
Outside clubs called Barbarella's
In the staff car park of estate agents
Two inches away from your car door
Alongside the contents of emptied ashtrays
On an advertising hoarding
On a double yellow line outside a wine bar
In the out-patients' car park

Where are you, Sir Bob? Ten charities for the 1990s

DisplAID (for destitute window dressers)
WaylAID (for those bothered by insurance brokers)
FlAID (for compromised Scottish judges)
UnderpAID (for ambulancemen)
PlAID (for unemployed clothmakers)
StockAID (for record producers who have run out of ideas)
StAID (for dull people)
ArcAID (for beleaguered shopping centre owners)
LemonAID (for alcoholics)
DelAID (for airline passengers)

Fashion-speak: a guide to interpretation

Unstructured: Creased
Executive-style: Suit
Investment wardrobe: Several suits
Comfortable: Shapeless
Classic: Black dress
Daring: Unwearable
Understated: Dull
Street style: Would look good on a road sweeper
Warm colours: Various shades of brown
Ethnic: Swathed in yards of hand-printed cotton

The essential guide to Christmas survival

Tell the in-laws you're spending Christmas Day with your parents

Tell your parents you're spending Christmas Day with the in-laws

Tell everyone else you're going away

Don't buy any toys that say 'Easy to assemble'

Turn all the lights off when carol singers are in your street

Dig out that old newspaper cutting about how to cook turkey properly

Wear protective goggles when trying to crack brazil nuts

Volunteer to go in to the office on Boxing Day

Use your Christmas pudding for display purposes only

Don't turn the TV on until at least 10 a.m.

Ten Christmas Day nightmares

Cooking sherry before lunch

Turning on the TV to find Su Pollard going round a children's hospital

Being sent out to find a shop which is open *and* sells batteries

Someone buying the kids a Little Drummer kit

Still waiting for the turkey to defrost at 5 p.m.

'Fun' underwear

Getting stuck with the dark meat

Being forced to wear the hat out of your cracker

No choice other than *The Great Escape* or *The Dirty Dozen*

Someone counting the 'units' of alcohol you've had

Ten things you'll regret buying in the January sales

A family of glass elephants
A red satin cushion shaped like Mick Jagger's lips
A fluffy Grenadier Guard tidybin
A one-inch Wedgwood cup and saucer set
An antique-style TV and video cabinet
A reproduction Roman legionnaire's helmet
Cork-backed table mats featuring hunting scenes
Christmas decorations for next year
A brass-look standard lamp in the shape of a palm tree
Anything that 'folds away conveniently'

New Age-speak: a guide to interpretation

Holistic: Not going to the doctor
Natural tonic: Water
Stress management: Not working
Traditional remedy: Last used when life expectancy was thirty
    years
Sustainable economy: Living in a tepee
Vitality dict: Salad
Fashion: Any colour as long as it's white
Fashion accessory: Children
Ley-line: Flying saucer runway
Change of life: Getting a new crystal

Arts theatre-speak: a guide to interpretation

Experimental: Audience faces away from the stage
Relevant: *Julius Caesar* set in the Stock Exchange
Subsidised: Everything apart from the bar
Cabaret: Two men, two women and an old upright piano
Fringe: Juggling as a political statement
Visual arts: Exhibition of out-of-focus photographs in the
    foyer
Music: An evening with Nicaragua's leading folk singer
Children's theatre: *Jack and the Organically-Grown Beanstalk*
Populist: It's okay to enjoy something once in a while
Provocative: One-woman show about life on a new town
    housing estate

Ten things you can never find

The takeaway menu for the local Indian restaurant
The telephone code book
Expensive fountain pens
One of the letters in a Scrabble set
The roll of Sellotape
Guarantees for appliances which go wrong
Your passport
Instruction booklets
The last piece of a jigsaw puzzle
Children when it's their bedtime

Ten reasons to avoid New Year's Eve parties

They're full of people smoking themselves silly before giving
  up
You made a resolution last year never to go to another one
You can't leave before midnight
You only know the first line of *Auld Lang Syne*
All that kissing could be dangerous
You have no opinions about the past year
There might be a copy of *Donald Where's Your Troosers?*
Somebody's bound to make a fool of themselves, and it might
  be you
You won't have recovered from Christmas
You wouldn't be able to look another sausage-on-a-stick in
  the face

Agony aunt-speak: a guide to interpretation

Write in complete confidence: To me and six million readers
Try surprising him: Do the housework with nothing on
It's a very common complaint: Especially if you're very
    common
Have you thought of evening classes?: They're packed with
    social inadequates like you
You're playing with fire: What you're doing is immoral and
    very possibly illegal

You need professional help: Get the best divorce lawyer
    available
I'm afraid I can't answer letters personally: I've got my own
    problems, you know
Try to see his point of view: You're the one to blame
Laugh and joke with each other: Impotence has its positive
    side
You must see your doctor immediately: Yuk!

Is it junk mail? Ten tell-tale signs

Your name is spelt wrongly
It says 'Printed in the Netherlands'
There's a 5p piece stuck to it
It refers to 'You and your family' even if you're single
There's no postmark
It suggests you could win £250,000
It promises that you have definitely won a consolation prize
The envelope has a little window in it
It looks remarkably similar to something which arrived two
        weeks earlier
It says 'This is not a circular'

Ten modern medical complaints

Passive smoker's cough
Couch potato's bottom
Channel flicker's finger
Sunday Times back strain
Tap-water tummy
Commuter's catatonia
Homeowner's depression
Rapper's throat
Politician's flatulence
M25 blood pressure

There's no business like snow business – a guide to ski resorts

Excellent safety record: No snow
Traditional nightlife: Satellite TV in every room
Favoured by the jet set: Somebody thinks they once spotted
    Robert Wagner
Record winter sunshine: Avalanches
Friendly locals: Usually called Heidi
Chalet maids: Sloane Rangers who can't cook
Outstanding walks: No ski lifts
Perfect for beginners: Flat
Enjoy the Tyrolean evenings: Get drunk
Fairytale forests: Plenty of trees to crash into

School reports: a guide to interpretation

Could do better: Couldn't do any worse
Prefers his own company: Needs a bath
Popular with classmates: Too much pocket money
Pays close attention: Copies from other children
Shows initiative: Steals the answer books
Prefers to work unsupervised: Plays truant
Could go far: The farther the better
Takes a pride in her work: Show-off
Mature, outgoing personality: Popular behind the bike sheds
Has made a real effort: Came second from bottom instead of
    bottom

A handy guide to pub guides

Traditional: Painted in essence of nicotine
Beer garden: Hanging baskets in the car park
Popular with locals: Remember *Straw Dogs*?
Lively atmosphere: Fights at the weekend
Home-cooked food: That's what it says on the packet
Unspoiled: Outside toilets
Good facilities: Inside toilets, occasionally with loo paper
Children welcome: Try the next pub
Live music: Can't hear yourself speak
Real ale: Lots of men wearing chunky-knit sweaters and
    beards

Ten things you never imagined you'd do when you were young

Go to bed before ten o'clock
Voluntarily eat sprouts
Spend more money on your parents' birthday presents than
  they do on yours
Complain about 'young people today'
Find conversations about curtains interesting

Hate funfairs
Watch TV every night
Buy sensible shoes
Listen to Radio 2
Worry about money

Are you a right clever dick? Ten tell-tale signs

You know all the best buys in this month's *Which?*
You can re-fold a map perfectly
You service your own car
You were always suspicious of microwave ovens
You can re-pack your suitcase at the end of a holiday
You sing hymns without a hymn book
Your sauces never curdle
You passed your driving test first time
You can re-set a digital watch in less than an hour
You can work out how many points are needed to finish a
    darts game

Left-wing-speak: a guide to interpretation

Bourgeois: Using coloured toilet paper
Proletarian art: Graffiti
Elitist: Someone who corrects your spelling
Class warfare: Stealing from Sainsbury's
Bourgeois individualism: Crying
Ruling class ideology: Highway code
Fascist: Anyone who disagrees with you
Capitalist press: Fails to report SWP branch meetings
Sexism: Watching *Terry and June*
Class victim: Laughing at *Terry and June*

Ten new gadgets for a Swiss Army knife

An escargot fork
A water purifier
An egg separator
A satellite TV decoder
A spike to keep petrol coupons on
A key for opening sardine tins
A secondary smoking detector
A thing for getting jammed coins out of public phones
A shrink-wrap remover
Barbecue tongs

Are you a New Man? Ten tell-tale signs

You wish you looked like William Hurt
You think breathing is something you do at ante-natal classes
You are relaxed about the fact that your GP is a woman
You read Virago Modern Classics
You can see Julie Burchill's point of view about men
You don't restrict your culinary efforts to the annual barbecue
You get excited by shopping
You'd rather see *Three Men and A Baby* than *Indiana Jones and the Last Crusade*
You think of alcohol in terms of 'units'
You're worried that there's a growing backlash against the New Man

Job references: a guide to interpretation

Reliable and hardworking: Saddled with a huge mortgage
Pleasant personality: Thick
Executive potential: Watch your back
Good telephone manner: Sloane Ranger
Lively: Shouts down the phone
Flexible: Happy to do all the boring jobs
Conscientious: Doesn't spend ages in the loo
Confident: Answers back
Creative: Doodles on invoices
Loyal: Tells tales on workmates

Ten things women find easier to do than men

Get elected Prime Minister
Admit they don't understand a joke
Dance with members of their own sex
Drive slowly
Remember who wore what at yesterday's party
Remember who wore what at a party five years ago
Eat oranges in bed
Write letters to friends
Complain in shops
Wrap presents

Ten things men find easier to do than women

End a telephone conversation
Drink from cans
Shower together after sports
Tell jokes
Leave the dishes until the morning
Hold on to go to the loo
Go into pubs on their own
Ignore the horoscope page
Marry people shorter than them
Open screw-top bottles

A dictionary of comedy

Alternative: Alternative to humour
Cult: At least someone found it funny
Ethnic: Lenny Henry telling a mother-in-law joke
Fringe: Beyond most people
Satirical: Bringing the house down merely by saying 'Thatch'
Silent: Mime artist in front of an audience who don't laugh
Situation: Perpetuates the myth that the local vicar often pops
        round
Pythonesque: Anything which isn't a sitcom
Stand-up: Or if you're Dave Allen, sit-down
Surreal: The only explanation for Little and Large

The ten laws of air travel

The closer you get to the airport, the greater the worry that you forgot to lock the back door

Nobody has ever been known to read the terms and conditions on their ticket

All mirrors in aircraft toilets make you look ill

Food trays are always fuller after you've finished eating

Sleeping on planes makes your mouth taste horrible

Hand luggage small enough to fit under the seat has not been invented

The duty-free trolley is designed to impede progress to and from the loo

People still think that if they stand up as soon as the aircraft comes to a halt, they'll be able to get off more quickly

There is no solution for people carrying sombreros

The more nonchalant you are going through customs, the more guilty you'll look

A.S.T.A. APPROVED
TWO PIECE
TRAVEL SOMBRERO

IDEAL FOR THE FREQUENT
- AIR TRAVELLER.

Ten places to avoid if you don't want to lose your credibility

Restaurants where fish dishes come under the menu heading
     'From the net'
Shops with names like Gift Ideas 'N' Things
Anything which calls itself a 'fayre'
Studio audiences for game shows
The book department of Woolworth's
A Rubettes' revival tour
Pubs with 'Duck Or Grouse' signs
Bar-B-Qs (as opposed to barbecues)
The queue for a Jeffrey Archer play
Behind Esther Rantzen on *That's Life*

The national curriculum at a glance

Geography: Shopping surveys
Business studies: Typing
Economics: Adding up grocery bills
Sociology: Discussing *Neighbours*
Media studies: Watching adverts
English language: Reading the papers
English literature: *Adrian Mole*
Religious studies: Chance for teacher to mark homework
History: Trip to see *Born on the 4th of July*
Chemistry: Dropping coins into beakers of Coke

Those social classifications explained

A: You shop in places where the goods don't have price tags
B: You know someone who once read *The Independent* magazine all the way through
C1: You gave up drinking Hirondelle some time ago
C2: You put in your own patio
D: You've got furry dice in your car
E: You're saving up to buy some furry dice
F1: You put your son's name down at birth for Eton Jobcentre
F2: You pay the community charge on your cardboard box
G: You have a subscription to *Sunday Sport*
H: You work for *Sunday Sport*

Ten things which always happen in the aftermath of a disaster

The emergency services 'respond magnificently'
The Queen sends a message conveying her 'distress'
The Prime Minister visits the scene
The Duchess of York is on holiday
There are calls for a 'full independent inquiry'
Newspaper columnists who were not present describe what happened and cite individual acts of bravery
The Labour Party says that now is not the time to make political points
The Labour Party makes political points
The Minister responsible says, 'You may be sure that something will be done'
Nothing is done

The ten laws of summer

Heatwaves always start on the day you go abroad

However early you light the barbecue, it never gets going
until after dark

The waistband of your shorts mysteriously shrinks over the
winter

If the filter breaks down at the local swimming pool, it's the
hottest day of the year

Complaints about having to water the lawn are equalled only
by complaints about not being able to water it because
of a hosepipe ban

After a day at the coast, everyone sets off for home at the
same time to avoid the traffic

The practice of picnics never lives up to the theory

The level of rainfall is directly proportional to the level of
noise the kids make in the house

The Jungle Book will be showing at a cinema near you

At the first sign of rain, someone is always on hand to say,
'Well, I suppose that was summer then'

Post-feminism: a guide to interpretation

Post-feminist: Career woman who wants to get married
The other woman: The nanny
Feminism: Blame Germaine Greer
Equality: He wears the earrings
The new celibacy: Having children
Career incentives: Mortgage interest rates
The new man: He shares your Body Shop face mask
Fashion: Skirts can be fun
Philosophy: Men and women are different
Sharing: First one home puts the M&S meal into the oven

Ten things we'd rather not see in the 1990s

Another Fish Called Wanda
Another Fish Called Michael
Kenneth Branagh in a new Dennis Potter series
More books of Marilyn Monroe pictures
Advertising campaigns for privatisation
Floyd On Indigestion
Low-alcohol louts
Richard Branson ballooning through the hole in the ozone
    layer
A comeback tour by the Osmonds
More Sunday newspapers

So you want to be alone? Ten ways to keep the neighbours at bay

Invite them in for a cheese and non-alcoholic wine party
Paint your house orange and purple
Put a 'Friends of the Aerosol' poster in the window
Fill the front garden with old prams and motorcycle spares
Apply for planning permission to build an outside toilet
Lobby the local council to change your street name to
     'F. W. de Klerk Way'
Tell everyone that you're better off under the Poll Tax
Start a Rottweiler Owners' Club
Never open your curtains
Put a Comic Relief red nose on your front door

How times change – ten things you wouldn't have thought possible ten years ago

The Green Party would be taken seriously
Eric Clapton would be on *Desert Island Discs*
We wouldn't want to bathe on our beaches
The Berlin Wall would bring people together
Steve Ovett would cry when offered money
The mini-skirt would make a comeback
Wimbledon FC would win the Cup Final
Half the people you know would be shareholders
Bowls would be a major sport on TV
Australian soap operas would be bigger than *Dallas*

Ten things children can do that their parents can't

Open child-proof medicine bottles
Programme the video machine
Eat sweets without getting fat
Name every American football quarterback
Sleep through thunderstorms
Find Roland Rat amusing
Think in metric measurements
Stay awake after 11 p.m.
Let white mice scamper all over them
Make £1 last for a whole week

Job ads: a guide to interpretation

Perfect opportunity for school-leavers: Pathetic pay

Pleasant working manner essential: Must be subservient

Salary negotiable: Downwards

Excellent travel opportunities: Sub-branch in Wolverhampton

Earn £££s: Sell double glazing

Enjoy working as part of a team: Join our typing pool

Earn money at home: Be exploited at home

Person Friday required: We're not sexist about who does the boring jobs

Must have sense of humour: Boss specialises in telling dirty jokes

All the advantages of a big company: Nobody knows anybody else's name

Films

Act your age – ten improbable parents

Sean Connery, 58, played the father of Harrison Ford, 46, in *Indiana Jones and the Last Crusade*

Angela Lansbury was 37 when she played the mother of 34-year-old Laurence Harvey in *The Manchurian Candidate*

In *Weeds*, Anne Ramsey, 58, plays the mother of Nick Nolte, 46

And in *Throw Momma from the Train*, Anne Ramsey, 58, plays the mother of Danny De Vito, 43

When Cary Grant made *North by Northwest*, he was 55. His mother, played by Jessie Royce Landis, was 54

Blair Brown and Mark Harmon were 39 and 36 when they played mother and son in *Stealing Home*

In *Beaches*, Lainie Kazan, 45, plays the mother of Bette Midler, 42

In *The Graduate*, Katharine Ross, who was 25, played the daughter of Anne Bancroft, 36

And in *The Colbys*, Katharine Ross, then 43, was the mother of John James, 29

Sean Connery, 58, played the father of Dustin Hoffman, 51, in *Family Business*

Ten actresses who tested for the part of Scarlett O'Hara

Lana Turner	Jean Harlow
Bette Davis	Carole Lombard
Loretta Young	Claudette Colbert
Norma Shearer	Katharine Hepburn
Joan Crawford	Ann Sheridan

Ten productions for ham actors

The Days of Swine and Roses
Porky and Bess
From Rasher With Love
All Quiet on the Western Runt
Barefoot in the Pork
The Old Curiosity Chop
The Pig Sleep
The Hogs of War
Lord of the Pies
Pigmalion

Ten films starring real-life married couples

Shanghai Surprise (Sean Penn and Madonna)
I Want a Divorce (Dick Powell and Joan Blondell)
The Reformer and the Redhead (Dick Powell and June Allyson)
Who's Afraid of Virginia Woolf? (Elizabeth Taylor and Richard Burton)
Go into Your Dance (Ruby Keeler and Al Jolson)
The Big Sleep (Lauren Bacall and Humphrey Bogart)
Witness for the Prosecution (Elsa Lanchester and Charles Laughton)
Modern Times (Charlie Chaplin and Paulette Goddard)
That Hamilton Woman (Vivien Leigh and Laurence Olivier)
The Lady from Shanghai (Orson Welles and Rita Hayworth)

Ten films for chocoholics

Mutiny on the Bounty (1935)
The Milky Way (1936)
Marathon Man (1976)
Galaxy of Terror (1981)
The Penguin Pool Murder (1932)
Taxi Driver (1976)
Picnic at Hanging Rock (1975)
The Lady and the Bandit (1951)
Trio (1950)
Invaders from Mars (1953)

It's an old cliché, but it might just work – ten Hollywood classics

Say, why don't we put the show on right here?
Wait a minute, boss – the kid can sing
Okay, you've got twenty-four hours – then we do it my way
All those years searching for happiness and here it was all the
     time, right under my nose
Give me the gun, son, and let's talk about it
Promise me you'll tell Mom that I died like a Brewster
It's an old trick, but it might just work
If I don't come back, will you take care of Jeannie and the
     kids?
And this time nobody's going to stand in my way, not even
     you
I guess I knew all along that it was you she really loved

Ten things which happen at every Oscar ceremony

Cher's outfit will reveal even more than it did the previous year

Woody Allen won't turn up

Someone very old indeed will shuffle on to a standing ovation

Steven Spielberg won't win anything

Someone will make an embarrassing political speech

Nobody will have heard of the Best Foreign Language Film

Every winner will thank at least three people

Every loser will smile and clap vigorously when the winners are announced

Britain will be able to claim some link with the Special Effects award

There'll be a special tribute to someone whose films appear only on BBC2 on Saturday afternoons

Ten films you must have in your video collection

Telephone Girl, Typist Girl, or Why I Became a Christian (India, 1925)

In My Time Boys Didn't Use Haircream (Argentina, 1937)

I-Ro-Ha-Ni-Ho-He-Yo (Japan, 1960)

Rat Fink A Boo Boo (USA, 1964)

The Nasty Rabbit (USA, 1965)

Ha Ha, Hee Hee, Hoo Hoo (India, 1955)

Why the UFOs Steal Our Lettuce (West Germany, 1979)

The Film that Rises to the Surface of Clarified Butter (USA, 1968)

Egg! Egg? (Sweden, 1975)

The Birth of New Zealand (New Zealand, 1922)

Ten films for football fans

The Groom Wore Spurs (1951)
The Petrified Forest (1936)
Villa Rides (1968)
The City (1939)
The Texas Rangers (1936)
Reds (1981)
The Sea Wolves (1980)
Kind Hearts and Coronets (1949)
The Arsenal Stadium Mystery (1939)
The Wrecking Crewe (1968)

Ten beastly Oscar winners

The Lion in Winter (1968): Best actress (Katharine Hepburn)
The Deer Hunter (1978): Best film
Raging Bull (1980): Best actor (Robert De Niro)
Save the Tiger (1973): Best actor (Jack Lemmon)
Who Framed Roger Rabbit (1988): Best visual effects
Cat Ballou (1965): Best actor (Lee Marvin)
To Kill a Mockingbird (1962): Best actor (Gregory Peck)
One Flew Over the Cuckoo's Nest (1975): Best film
The Kiss of the Spider Woman (1985): Best actor (William
    Hurt)
A Fish Called Wanda (1988): Best supporting actor (Kevin
    Kline)

Ten movie prequels waiting to be made

Thursday the Twelfth
Undercoat Your Wagon
The Draughtsman's Estimate
Daydream on Elm Street
Friday Night and Saturday Morning
The Undergraduate
The Catering Student, the Juvenile Offender, His Girlfriend
    and Her Chum
Guess Who's Coming to Tea?
Kramer Marries Kramer
The Godson Part One

Ten real-life relationships translated to the screen

Margaux and Mariel Hemingway: sisters in *Lipstick*
Dennis and Randy Quaid: brothers in *The Long Riders*
James and Jeanne Cagney: brother and sister in *Yankee Doodle Dandy*
Diane Cilento and Jason Connery: mother and son in *The Boy Who Had Everything*
Priscilla Pointer and Amy Irving: mother and daughter in *Carrie*
Raymond and Daniel Massey: father and son in *The Queen's Guards*
Michael and Vanessa Redgrave: father and daughter in *Behind The Mask*
Madhur and Sakeena Jaffrey: mother and daughter in *The Perfect Murder*
Geoffrey and Felicity Kendal: father and daughter in *Shakespeare Wallah*
Martin and Gary Kemp: twins in *The Krays*

Ten movie remakes for the 1990s

A Fistful of ECUs
How Green Was My Manifesto
Above Us The Raw Sewage
Reach For The Hole In The Ozone Layer
The Community Charge Of The Light Brigade
One Hundred And One Rottweilers
War And Greenpeace
Invasion Of The Liver And Kidney Snatchers
Centigrade 232
Maggie – A Suitable Case For Treatment

Those who are about to die . . . ten movie lines which tell you someone's about to be bumped off

'Let's split up and I'll search the cellar'
'Of course I'll marry you, 007'
'Why did you bring me all the way up here?'
'I'm getting out of this place first thing in the morning'
'Hello, operator, I've been cut off – hello, operator?'
'Oh, it's only you – come in'
'Why are you looking at me like that?'
'Don't worry, you're safe now'
'So it was you all along'
'There's no way anyone can get in now'

Ten actors who have played themselves in movies

Humphrey Bogart: *The Love Lottery* (1953)
Henry Fonda: *Fedora* (1978)
Orson Welles: *Follow the Boys* (1944)
Charlie Chaplin: *Show People* (1929)
Frank Sinatra: *Cannonball Run II* (1983)
Larry Hagman: *I Am Blushing* (1981)
Bing Crosby: *Let's Make Love* (1960)
Martin Sheen: *The King of Prussia* (1982)
Sid James: *The Beauty Contest* (1964)
Ronald Reagan: *It's a Great Feeling* (1949)

Ten actresses who have played themselves in movies

Anne Bancroft: *Silent Movie* (1976)
Bette Davis: *Hollywood Canteen* (1944)
Julie Christie: *Nashville* (1975)
Gloria Swanson: *Airport* (1974)
Katharine Hepburn: *Stage Door Canteen* (1943)
Dorothy Lamour: *Duffy's Tavern* (1945)
Liv Ullman: *Players* (1979)
Natalie Wood: *Willie and Phil* (1981)
Susannah York: *Long Shot* (1978)
Liza Minelli: *The Muppets Take Manhattan* (1984)

You've got to start somewhere – ten roles stars would probably prefer to forget

Clint Eastwood's first role was as a lab technician in *Revenge of the Creature* (1955)

Harrison Ford made his debut as a bellboy in *Dead Heat on a Merry-Go-Round* (1966)

Jane Fonda made her film debut as a cheerleader in *Tall Story* (1960)

Robert Vaughn played the title role in *Teenage Caveman* (1958)

Jack Nicholson played a masochistic dental patient in *The Little Shop of Horrors* (1961)

Sean Connery was a diamond scavenger in *Tarzan's Greatest Adventure* (1959)

Donald Sutherland made his debut in a dual role: as a soldier and (in drag) as a witch in *Castle of the Living Dead* (1964)

Debra Winger played Lynda Carter's younger sister in the TV series *Wonder Woman* (1976)

Charles Bronson played a grotesque deaf-mute in *House of Wax* (1953)

Mel Gibson's first role was as a surfer in *Summer City* (1976)

Ten actors who won only honorary Oscars

Fred Astaire	Greta Garbo
Edward G. Robinson	Groucho Marx
Judy Garland	Shirley Temple
Bob Hope	Cary Grant
Gene Kelly	Danny Kaye

Where Hollywood meets Fleet Street

The Guardian (1984)
Von Ryan's Express (1965)
Crack in the Mirror (1960)
The Man Without a Star (1955)
Mail Order Bride (1963)
Hard Times (1975)
People on Sunday (1929)
Greed in the Sun (1964)
Foreign Correspondent (1940)
The Single Standard (1929)

Ten Indiana Jones *films still on the drawing board*

Indiana Jones and the Last Bus to Barnsley
Indiana Jones and the Missing Pink Frock
Indiana Jones and the Cordon Bleu Cookery Course
Indiana Jones and the Multiple Share Application
Indiana Jones and the Wife's Mother's Hat
Indiana Jones and the Winning Premium Bond
Indiana Jones and the Seven-Day Diet
Indiana Jones and the Weekend Shopping Expedition
Indiana Jones and the Unfortunate Haircut
Indiana Jones and the Self-Catering Holiday

Ten actresses who were beauty queens

Sylvia Kristel (Miss Television Europe, 1973)
Cybill Shepherd (Miss Teenage Memphis, 1966)
Michelle Pfeiffer (Miss Orange County, 1976)
Kim Novak (Miss Deepfreeze, 1953)
Raquel Welch (Miss Photogenic, 1953)
Dyan Cannon (Miss West Seattle, 1957)
Sophia Loren (Miss Elegance, 1950)
Claudia Cardinale (The Most Beautiful Italian Girl in Tunis, 1956)
Lauren Bacall (Miss Greenwich Village, 1942)
Debbie Reynolds (Miss Burbank, 1948)

It's the way they sell 'em – classic lines used to promote films

'In space, no one can hear you scream!' (*Alien*)
'They're young . . . they're in love . . . and they kill people!' (*Bonnie and Clyde*)
'Just when you thought it was safe to go back in the water' (*Jaws 2*)
'There are three sides to this love story' (*Kramer v Kramer*)
'We are not alone . . .' (*Close Encounters of the Third Kind*)
'You don't assign him to murder cases – you just turn him loose!' (*Dirty Harry*)
'Love means never having to say you're sorry' (*Love Story*)
'To have seen it is to wear a badge of courage!' (*Frankenstein*)
'A love story every woman would die a thousand deaths to live!' (*Jane Eyre*)
'This is Benjamin . . . he's a little worried about his future!' (*The Graduate*)

The ten most filmed stories

Cinderella
Hamlet
Carmen
Faust
Doctor Jekyll and Mr Hyde

Romeo and Juliet
Robinson Crusoe
La Dame Aux Camélias
Don Quixote
The Three Musketeers

A fruit salad of films

The Greengage Summer
Wild Strawberries
A Clockwork Orange
Bananas
The Apple Dumpling Gang

Watermelon Man
Eat the Peach
Can She Bake a Cherry Pie?
The Lemon Drop Kid
The Grapes of Wrath

Reviving the British film industry – ten remakes to get us going

The Mancunian Candidate
Meet Me in St Alban's
The Bridge on the River Wye
Bad Day at Blackpool Rock
The Life and Times of Judge
    James Pickles

Our Man in Havant
Ron Brown's Schooldays
Song of Norwood
The Greatest Tory Ever Sold
All Quiet on the Western
    Bypass

'This one's for Johnny . . .': ten films that made him famous

Johnny Angel (1945)
Johnny Cool (1963)
Johnny Concho (1956)
Johnny Trouble (1956)
Johnny Eager (1942)

Johnny Guitar (1953)
Johnny Dangerously (1984)
Johnny Dark (1954)
Johnny Nobody (1960)
Johnny Handsome (1989)

Ten things we know about America from watching the movies

Nobody ever eats more than one mouthful from a plate of food

Every platoon has at least one person who can play the mouth-organ

All young boys can reach their bedroom by climbing a convenient tree

Restaurants offer at least six different kinds of toast for breakfast

Nobody ever locks their car

The bedroom curtains are always left open at night

If there's a storm, the bedroom window is left open as well

Everybody goes to school until the age of thirty

When people fall in love they go shopping in the local street market

Paper boys never need to get off their bicycles

Ten movie stars who have been played by movie stars

Joan Crawford (Faye Dunaway in *Mommie Dearest*)

W. C. Fields (Rod Steiger in *W. C. Fields and Me*)

Buster Keaton (Donald O'Connor in *The Buster Keaton Story*)

Jean Harlow (Carroll Baker in *Harlow*)

Frances Farmer (Jessica Lange in *Frances*)

Carole Lombard (Jill Clayburgh in *Gable and Lombard*)

Rudolph Valentino (Franco Nero in *The Legend of Valentino*)

Lon Chaney Snr (James Cagney in *The Man of a Thousand Faces*)

John Barrymore (Errol Flynn in *Too Much Too Soon*)

Bruce Lee (Bruce Li in *Bruce Lee – the True Story*)

Take one – ten childish film debuts of movie stars

Beau Bridges appeared in *No Minor Vices* (1948) aged seven
Jeff Bridges appeared in *The Company She Keeps* (1949) aged two
Natalie Wood appeared in *Happy Land* (1943) aged five
Rita Moreno appeared in *Silk Legs* (1936) aged five
Ron Howard appeared in *The Journey* (1958) aged five
Liza Minelli appeared in *In the Good Old Summertime* (1949) aged three
Bruce Lee appeared in *The Birth of Mankind* (1946) aged six
Jodie Foster appeared in *Napoleon and Samantha* (1971) aged eight
Juliet Mills appeared in *In Which We Serve* (1941) aged one
Cyril Cusack appeared in *Knocknagow* (1918) aged eight

'Aren't you on the wrong side of the camera?' Ten directors who have appeared in movies

Steven Spielberg (*The Blues Brothers*)
Martin Scorsese (*Pavlova – a Woman for All Time*)
Bob Fosse (*The Little Prince*)
Lindsay Anderson (*Chariots of Fire*)
François Truffaut (*Close Encounters of the Third Kind*)
John Boorman (*Long Shot*)
Sydney Pollack (*Tootsie*)
Martin Ritt (*The End of the Game*)
Roman Polanski (*Chinatown*)
Elia Kazan (*Blues in the Night*)

Sport

Over the moon, or sick as a parrot – ten sports stars who have cried in public

Tony Jacklin after winning the 1987 Ryder Cup

Steve Davis after winning the 1983 World Snooker Championship

Kim Hughes after resigning as Australia's cricket captain in 1984

Tessa Sanderson as she limped away injured from the 1986 Olympic trials

Jocky Wilson after winning the 1982 Embassy World Darts Championship

Mary Decker after tripping over Zola Budd's heels in the 1984 Olympics

Jack Nicklaus after winning his first British Open in 1966

Steve Ovett after the 1500 metres final at the 1989 Commonwealth Games trials

Fatima Whitbread after winning gold at the 1986 European Championships

Paul Gascoigne after playing West Germany in the semi-finals of the 1990 World Cup

Ten soccer trialists

Eddie Large (Manchester City)
Rod Stewart (Brentford)
Julio Iglesias (Real Madrid)
Mike Gatting (Arsenal)
Des O'Connor (Northampton Town)
Boris Becker (Bayern Munich)
Billy Cotton Snr (Brentford)
Stan Boardman (Liverpool)
David Essex (Leyton Orient)
Dr Robert of the Blow Monkeys (Norwich City)

Soccer players' form: a guide to interpretation

Good footballing brain: Brain like a football
Competitive: Dirty
Seasoned professional: Over the hill
Loyal club player: Never been approached by another club
Creative: Namby-pamby
Not afraid to take people on: Always arguing about his
    contract
Individualist: Wears shirt outside his shorts
Two-footed: Misses scoring chances with both feet
Terrier-like: Short midfielder who runs himself ragged
Dangerous in the box: Scores own goals

A guide to Dan Maskell-speak

Ooh, I say: Everybody is entitled to a catchphrase

What a dream shot: This gives you an idea of what I dream about

This man really is a Centre Court favourite: He loses graciously every year

McEnroe seems a little upset by that decision: The umpire is being given first aid

A wonderful performance by the Englishman: He lost in four sets instead of three

What a marvellous cross-court, forehand volley on the run: I do know what I'm talking about

He is a true gentleman: He's the only player not covered in advertisements

And the crowd are enjoying this bit of light relief: Lendl has offered his racket to a ballboy

Even on the replay, it's difficult to judge: It was definitely out, but I don't believe in arguing with the umpire

Can the English girl do anything to keep her hopes alive?: Can I do anything to keep the viewers' interest alive?

An England cricket eleven to take on the World (all born abroad and all qualified to play)

Gehan Mendis (Sri Lanka)

Chris Smith (South Africa)

Robin Smith (South Africa)

Allan Lamb (South Africa)

Roland Butcher (Barbados)

Nasser Hussain (India)

Ian Greig (South Africa)

Phil De Freitas (Dominica)

Rajesh Maru (Kenya)

Gladstone Small (Barbados)

Devon Malcolm (Jamaica)

Ten towns which used to have Football League clubs

Gateshead
Durham
Newport
Barrow
Colchester

Workington
Southport
Merthyr Tydfil
Nelson
Accrington

Play up, play up and play the game – ten unlikely athletes

Winston Churchill was Public Schools' Foils Champion in 1892

Johnny Mathis was ranked eighty-fifth in the world at high jump in 1955

Dr Benjamin Spock was a member of the 1924 American Olympic rowing team

Sir Arthur Conan Doyle played cricket for the MCC and once bowled out W. G. Grace

Idi Amin won the heavyweight boxing championship of Uganda in 1951 and successfully defended it for nine years

Lady Docker was the unofficial women's world marbles champion in 1955

Albert Camus was the first-team goalkeeper for Oran FC in Algeria

Lord Byron captained the Harrow cricket team

John Paul Getty was an undefeated amateur boxer who once knocked out Jack Dempsey in a bar-room brawl

Wyatt Earp refereed a world championship boxing match between Bob Fitzsimmons and Tom Sharkey in 1896

FA Cup-speak: a guide to interpretation

We wouldn't mind being drawn against Manchester United:
We wouldn't mind making a lot of money

We'd be happy just to force a replay: We'd be happy to
double our money

We're relying on our fans to lift us: We're playing Liverpool

The whole town is buzzing: Children are being evacuated and
shops are being boarded up

On the day, it's 11 against 11: 11 no-hopers against 11
internationals

Anything can happen: But probably won't

We're relying on a good Cup run: We're staring relegation in
the face

The club is no stranger to giant-killing: Who can forget 1922?

The Cup is a great leveller: That's our only hope – levelling
their strikers

We're just going out to enjoy ourselves: We've got no chance

Ten sports stars who made records

Tony Jacklin: *The Lincolnshire Poacher*
Kevin Keegan: *Head over Heels*
Jocky Wilson and Bobby George: *One Hundred and Eighty*
Brian Clough: *You Can't Win Them All*
Terry Venables: *What Do You Want to Make Those Eyes at Me
For*
Alex Higgins: *One Four Seven*
Donald Bradman: *Bungalow of Dreams*
Glen Hoddle and Chris Waddle: *Diamond Lights*
Jo Durie: *Wimbledon Lawns*
Henry Cooper: *Knock Me Down with a Feather*

The other BAFTA – ten British Academy of Football Television Awards

Most convincing dive in the penalty area
Best supporting crowd
Most original off-the-ball incident
Most spectacular collision with a cameraman
The Bobby Robson Memorial Award for best excuse in defeat
The Motson Award for best pronunciation of the Yugoslavian
    team
Best use of cliché in a post-match interview
Best use of animation in an argument with the referee
Most embarrassingly audible crowd chant
Best George

Think European – an England soccer eleven for 1992

John Lukic (Leeds)
Francis Benali (Southampton)
Graham Le Saux (Chelsea)
Martin Kuhl (Portsmouth)
Scott Minto (Charlton)
Alan Paris (Leicester)
Robert Rosario (Norwich)
Imre Varadi (Leeds)
Marco Gabbiadini (Sunderland)
Matthew Le Tissier (Southampton)
Giuliano Maiorana (Manchester United)

'Quite extraordinary' – World Cup facts to bore your friends with

The original 1966 World Cup commemorative stamp was
  scrapped because it showed the flag of North Korea, a
  country Britain didn't recognise

In the fourteen tournaments, the host country has won five
  times

Honduras and El Salvador went to war as a result of a
  qualifying tie in 1969

Brazil is the only country to have appeared in every one of the
  finals

In 1974, Ernest Jean-Joseph of Haiti became the first player
  to be banned for taking drugs

The USA has appeared in the finals four times, reaching the
  semis in 1930

Mario Zagalo of Brazil and Franz Beckenbauer of West
  Germany are the only men to have won the finals first
  as a player and then as team manager

Norman Whiteside of Northern Ireland is the youngest player
  to have appeared in the finals, when he was seventeen,
  in 1982

Hungary is the only team to have scored ten goals, when they
  beat El Salvador 10–1 in 1982

Just Fontaine of France holds the record for scoring the most
  goals in the finals – thirteen in 1958

Ten England cricket captains who weren't born in England

Tony Greig (South Africa)

Colin Cowdrey (India)

Lord Harris (Trinidad)

Douglas Jardine (India)

Gubby Allen (Australia)

Pelham Warner (Trinidad)

Freddie Brown (Peru)

Ted Dexter (Italy)

Mike Denness (Scotland)

Tony Lewis (Wales)

Ten movies for sports personalities

Drive, He Said (Nick Faldo)
Black Narcissus (Carl Lewis)
Outrageous Fortune (Chris Waddle)
The Wizard of Oz (Steve Waugh)
How to Get Ahead in Advertising (Daley Thompson)
Bringing Up Baby (John McEnroe)
The Wild One (David Bryant)
A Man for All Seasons (Desmond Lynam)
Superman (Graham Gooch)
The Lion in Winter (Mike Teague)

A guide to soccer's TV pundits

You've got to fancy the Brazilians: I'm taking no chances
He just doesn't seem to be able to produce his club form at
    national level: Yes, we're talking about John Barnes
The South Americans play a very different type of game: They
    score goals
Sweden versus Costa Rica looks like an interesting clash: We
    got stuck with televising it
There's no such thing as an easy match at this level: Get ready
    to be beaten by the Cameroons
I like the look of the Soviet number eight: I haven't a clue
    how to pronounce his name
That goalkeeper's a clown: I'm a graduate of the Brian
    Clough school of punditry
There's still forty-five minutes to go: It's half-time
This is the man many of us felt should have been in the side
    from the start: It's a substitute who's just made a decent
    pass
They'll be talking about this in the pubs tomorrow: No they
    won't – they'll be slumped in front of the telly watching
    more soccer

Ten batsmen dismissed by the first ball of a Test Match

Sunil Gavaskar (India *v* England, 1974)
Herbert Sutcliffe (England *v* New Zealand, 1932–3)
Roy Fredericks (West Indies *v* India, 1970–1)
Jim Morrison (New Zealand *v* England, 1974–5)
Eddie Barlow (South Africa *v* Australia, 1966–7)
Warren Bardsley (Australia *v* England, 1926)
Keith Stackpole (Australia *v* New Zealand, 1973–4)
Conrad Hunte (West Indies *v* Pakistan, 1957–8)
Tom Hayward (England *v* South Africa, 1907)
Sunil Gavaskar (India *v* West Indies, 1983–4)

'I minced it first time, Brian' – ten soccer players' former jobs

Chris Waddle (Marseilles): sausage-maker
Vinny Jones (Leeds United): hod-carrier
Steve Archibald (Español): mechanic
Alan Pardew (Crystal Palace): window-fitter
Phil Parkes (Ipswich Town): carpenter
Ian Wright (Crystal Palace): builder
Steve Bull (Wolves): warehouse worker
David Kelly (Leicester City): Cadbury's production-line
    worker
Pat Gavin (Gillingham): postman
Kerry Dixon (Chelsea): toolmaker

Ten reasons to look forward to the 1994 World Cup in America

Greavesie in a stetson
Commercial breaks after goals
Cheerleaders
Jack Nicholson in the crowd
Calvin Klein kits
The Big Mac Golden Goal competition
Team psychiatrists
The end of the 'Special Relationship'
Press conferences at half-time
Goalkeepers in helmets

Quotations

PLEASE DELIVER
TO THE
OXFORD DICTIONARY
OF QUOTATIONS

Cover your eyes! Ten quotes about sex

'I know nothing about sex because I was always married' (Zsa Zsa Gabor)

'I can't understand why more people aren't bisexual – it would double your chances for a date on Saturday night' (Woody Allen)

'Whoever named it necking was a poor judge of anatomy' (Groucho Marx)

'Sex is emotion in motion' (Mae West)

'I know it does make people happy, but to me it is just like having a cup of tea' (Cynthia Payne)

'To succeed with the opposite sex, tell her you're impotent – she can't wait to disprove it' (Cary Grant)

'Temptation is a woman's weapon and a man's excuse' (H. L. Mencken)

'Sex is the last refuge of the miserable' (Quentin Crisp)

'I feel like a million tonight – but one at a time' (Mae West)

'Sex – the poor man's polo' (Clifford Odets)

My philosophy – ten rules of life

'Start off every day with a smile and get it over with' (W. C. Fields)

'Husbands are like fires – they go out when unattended' (Cher)

'Only lie about the future' (Johnny Carson)

'If you want to be a success in life, just show up eighty per cent of the time' (Woody Allen)

'In a two-car family, the wife always has the smaller car' (Ruth Rendell)

'I'd rather have a free bottle in front of me than a prefrontal lobotomy' (Fred Allen)

'The nice thing about being a celebrity is that when you bore people they think it's their fault' (Henry Kissinger)

'They say ninety per cent of TV is junk – but ninety per cent of everything is junk' (Gene Roddenberry)

'You can pretend to be serious; you can't pretend to be witty' (Sacha Guitry)

'As a grown man you should know better than to go around advising people' (Bertolt Brecht)

Ten great put-downs

'That woman speaks eighteen languages and she can't say
  "No" in any of them' (Dorothy Parker)

'There's a lot to be said for being *nouveau riche* and the
  Reagans mean to say it all' (Gore Vidal)

'Working with her is like being hit over the head with a
  Valentine card' (Christopher Plummer on Julie
  Andrews)

'No, the "t" is silent, as in Harlow' (Margot Asquith to Jean
  Harlow when asked if the 't' was pronounced in
  Margot)

'She was the original good time that was had by all' (Bette
  Davis on a young starlet)

'Most of the time he sounds like he has a mouth full of wet
  toilet paper' (Rex Reed on Marlon Brando)

'Doris Day is as wholesome as a bowl of cornflakes and at
  least as sexy' (Dwight MacDonald)

'If you were my husband, I'd poison your coffee' (Nancy
  Astor). 'And if you were my wife, I'd drink it' (Winston
  Churchill)

'I could dance with you until the cows come home. On
  second thoughts, I'd rather dance with the cows till you
  come home' (Groucho Marx)

'She looked as if butter wouldn't melt in her mouth – or
  anywhere else' (Elsa Lanchester on Maureen O'Hara)

Ten views of men

'I like men to behave like men – strong and childish'
(Françoise Sagan)

'Macho does not prove mucho' (Zsa Zsa Gabor)

'The male is a domestic animal which, if treated with firmness
and kindness, can be trained to do most things' (Jilly
Cooper)

'No nice men are good at getting taxis' (Katherine
Whitehorn)

'You know the problem with men? After the birth, we're
irrelevant' (Dustin Hoffman)

'There are two things no man will admit he can't do well:
drive and make love' (Stirling Moss)

'Men have a much better time of it than women. For one
thing, they marry later. For another thing, they die
earlier' (H. L. Mencken)

'Men are those creatures with two legs and eight hands'
(Jayne Mansfield)

'Women want mediocre men and men are working to be as
mediocre as possible' (Margaret Mead)

'Men are beasts and even beasts don't behave as they do'
(Brigitte Bardot)

Ten views of women

'A woman is like a tea bag. You can't tell how strong she is
    until you put her in hot water' (Nancy Reagan)
'There are no ugly women, only lazy ones' (Helena
    Rubinstein)
'A woman's place is in the wrong' (James Thurber)
'Women are brighter than men, but it should be kept very
    quiet or it ruins the whole racket' (Anita Loos)
'Women over thirty are at their best, but men over thirty are
    too old to recognise it' (Jean-Paul Belmondo)
'The first time Adam had a chance, he laid the blame on
    women' (Nancy Astor)
'Women are nothing but machines for producing children'
    (Napoleon)
'There are only two kinds of women – goddesses and
    doormats' (Picasso)
'Women should be obscene and not heard' (John Lennon)
'The only really happy people are married women and single
    men' (H. L. Mencken)

Feeling your age? Ten quotes about growing old

'Old age isn't so bad when you consider the alternative' (John Masefield)

'I'm at that age now where just putting my cigar in its holder is a thrill' (George Burns)

'You're getting old when the girl you smile at thinks you're one of her father's friends' (Arthur Murray)

'Old age is when the narrow waist and the broad mind change places' (Patricia Moody)

'No man is really old until his mother stops worrying about him' (Bill Ryan)

'One of the many pleasures of old age is giving things up' (Malcolm Muggeridge)

'You know you're getting old when the candles cost more than the cake' (Bob Hope)

'I've reached that age in life where it is harder to find temptation than it is to resist it' (Edward E. Calhoun)

'I have everything I had twenty years ago – except now it's all lower' (Gypsy Rose Lee)

'Anyone can get old – all you have to do is to live long enough' (Groucho Marx)

Brought down in the aria – ten quotes about opera

'Opera is when a guy gets stabbed in the back and, instead of bleeding, he sings' (Ed Gardner)

'I do not mind what language an opera is sung in so long as it is a language I do not understand' (Sir Edward Appleton)

'No good opera plot can be sensible, for people do not sing when they are feeling sensible' (W. H. Auden)

'Oh, how wonderful, really wonderful, opera would be if there were no singers' (Rossini)

'People are wrong when they say the opera isn't what it used to be. It is what it used to be. That's what's wrong with it' (Noël Coward)

'The opera isn't over till the fat lady sings' (Dan Cook)

'One goes to see a tragedy to be moved; to the opera one goes either for want of any other interest or to facilitate digestion' (Voltaire)

'Going to the opera, like getting drunk, is a sin that carries its own punishment with it' (Hannah More)

'Opera is like a husband with a foreign title: expensive to support, hard to understand, and therefore a supreme social challenge' (Cleveland Amory)

'Opera in English is, in the main, just about as sensible as baseball in Italian' (H. L. Mencken)

Cheers! Ten quotes about drink

'I once shook hands with Pat Boone and my whole right side sobered up' (Dean Martin)

'One more drink and I'll be under the host' (Dorothy Parker)

'Pubs make you as drunk as they can as soon as they can, and turn nasty when they succeed' (Colin MacInnes)

'The trouble with the world is that everybody in it is three drinks behind' (Humphrey Bogart)

'An alcoholic is someone you don't like who drinks as much as you do' (Dylan Thomas)

'I drink to make other people interesting' (George Jean Nathan)

'A woman drove me to drink and I never even had the courtesy to thank her' (W. C. Fields)

'A man is never drunk if he can lie on the floor without holding on' (Joe E. Lewis)

'Maybe alcohol picks you up a little bit, but it sure lets you down in a hurry' (Betty Ford)

'My dad was the town drunk. A lot of times that's not so bad – but New York City?' (Henny Youngman)

Children – ten quotes about the little darlings

'The trouble with children is that they are not returnable' (Quentin Crisp)

'I love children – especially when they cry, for then someone takes them away' (Nancy Mitford)

'It is no wonder people are so horrible when they start life as children' (Kingsley Amis)

'Insanity is hereditary – you can get it from your children' (Sam Levenson)

'The thing that impresses me most about Americans is the way parents obey their children' (Duke of Windsor)

'Children are the most desirable opponents in Scrabble as they are both easy to beat and fun to cheat' (Fran Lebowitz)

'I love children – parboiled' (W. C. Fields)

'Do your kids a favour – don't have any' (Robert Orben)

'Children begin by loving their parents; after a time they judge them; rarely, if ever, do they forgive them' (Oscar Wilde)

'It is customarily said that Christmas is done for the kids – considering how awful Christmas is, and how little our society likes children, this must be true' (P. J. O'Rourke)

Rich man, poor man – ten quotes about wealth

'A man who has a million dollars is as well off as if he were rich' (J. J. Astor III)

'Lack of money is the root of all evil' (George Bernard Shaw)

'A fool and his money are soon married' (Carolyn Wells)

'The poor have more children, but the rich have more relatives' (Anon)

'I've been rich and I've been poor; rich is better' (Sophie Tucker)

'Money is like an arm or leg – use it or lose it' (Henry Ford)

'Money doesn't buy friends, but it allows a better class of enemy' (Lord Mancroft)

'Any man who has $10,000 left when he dies is a failure' (Errol Flynn)

'I must say I hate money, but it's the lack of it I hate most' (Katherine Mansfield)

'Money, it turned out, was exactly like sex – you thought of nothing else if you didn't have it, and thought of other things if you did' (James Baldwin)

The biter bit – ten quotes about critics

'Asking a working writer what he feels about critics is like asking a lamp-post what it feels about dogs' (John Osborne)

'Pay no attention to what the critics say – no statue has ever been put up to a critic' (Jean Sibelius)

'Critics can't even make music by rubbing their back legs together' (Mel Brooks)

'A drama critic is a man who leaves no turn unstoned' (George Bernard Shaw)

'Rock journalism is people who can't write interviewing people who can't talk for people who can't read' (Frank Zappa)

'Having the critics praise you is like having the hangman say you've got a pretty neck' (Eli Wallach)

'A critic is a man who knows the way but can't drive the car' (Kenneth Tynan)

'My mother – who was an alertly respectable woman – told me at an early age that I was not to play with critics' (Robert Bolt)

'Critics are like eunuchs in a harem: they know how it's done, they've seen it done every day, but they're unable to do it themselves' (Brendan Behan)

'Critics always want to put you into pigeon holes, which can be very uncomfortable unless you happen to be a pigeon' (Max Adrian)

Ten Oscar Wilde one-liners

Woman begins by resisting a man's advances and ends by blocking his retreat

Young men want to be faithful, and are not; old men want to be faithless, and cannot

To love oneself is the beginning of a lifelong romance

Nothing spoils a romance so much as a sense of humour in the woman – or the lack of it in a man

The old believe everything, the middle-aged suspect everything, the young know everything

Only people who look dull ever get into the House of Commons, and only people who are dull ever succeed there

Moderation is a fatal thing – nothing succeeds like excess

Every woman is a rebel, and usually in wild revolt against herself

Only dull people are brilliant at breakfast

Education is an admirable thing, but it is well to remember from time to time that nothing that is worth knowing can be taught

Stars and gripes – ten quotes about America

'America is the country where you buy a lifetime's supply of aspirin for one dollar and use it in two weeks' (John Barrymore)

'Americans like fat books and thin women' (Russell Baker)

'The trouble with America is that there are far too many wide open spaces surrounded by teeth' (Charles Luckman)

'America – a country that has leapt from barbarism to decadence without touching civilisation' (John O'Hara)

'It is absurd to say there are neither ruins nor curiosities in America when they have their mothers and their manners' (Oscar Wilde)

'In America you watch TV and think it's totally unreal – then you step outside and it's just the same' (Joan Armatrading)

'California is a great place – if you happen to be an orange' (Fred Allen)

'What a pity when Christopher Columbus discovered America that he ever mentioned it' (Margot Asquith)

'I've been a New Yorker for ten years, and the only people who are nice to us turn out to be Moonies' (P. J. O'Rourke)

'Nobody ever went broke underestimating the taste of the American public' (H. L. Mencken)

Ten quotes about actors, darling

'An actor is a guy who, if you aren't talking about him, isn't
listening' (Marlon Brando)

'I didn't say "actors are like cattle". I said "actors should be
treated like cattle"' (Alfred Hitchcock)

'A fan club is a group of people who tell an actor he is not
alone in the way he feels about himself' (Jack Carson)

'All actors are darlings backstage' (Bamber Gascoigne)

'Some of the greatest love affairs I've known involved one
actor, unassisted' (Wilson Mizner)

'You can pick out the actors by the glazed look that comes
into their eyes when the conversation wanders away
from themselves' (Michael Wilding)

'Actors and burglars work better at night' (Sir Cedric
Hardwicke)

'Very good actors never talk about their art. Very bad ones
never stop' (John Whiting)

'Most actresses just read their own lines to find out what
clothes they're going to wear' (Anita Loos)

'The best screen actor is that man who can do nothing
extremely well' (Alfred Hitchcock)

Marriage lines – ten quotes until death us do part

'A man in love is incomplete until he has married – then he's finished' (Zsa Zsa Gabor)

'Marriage is a wonderful invention; but then again so is a bicycle repair kit' (Billy Connolly)

'Marriage isn't a word – it's a sentence' (caption from King Vidor's silent film *The Crowd*)

'Marriage isn't a process of prolonging the life of love, but of mummifying the corpse' (P. G. Wodehouse and Guy Bolton)

'Marriage is the only war where one sleeps with the enemy' (Mexican proverb)

'I married beneath me – all women do' (Nancy Astor)

'When a man steals your wife, there is no better revenge than to let him keep her' (Sacha Guitry)

'Marriage is like life in this: it is a field of battle and not a bed of roses' (Robert Louis Stevenson)

'A wedding is just a happy funeral' (Paul Theroux)

'Marriage is the result of the longing for the deep, deep peace of the double bed after the hurly-burly of the chaise longue' (Mrs Patrick Campbell)

Ten views of success

'Behind every successful man stands an amazed woman'
(Anon)

'Success to me is having ten honeydew melons and only
eating the top half of each one' (Barbra Streisand)

'If you become a success, you don't change – everyone else
does' (Kirk Douglas)

'If at first you don't succeed, try, try again. Then quit. There's
no use being a damned fool about it' (W. C. Fields)

'The worst part of having success is to try finding someone
who is happy for you' (Bette Midler)

'Success is being nothing but a quote' (Andy Partridge)

'We must believe in luck, for how else can we explain the
success of those we don't like?' (Jean Cocteau)

'It is not enough to succeed. Others must fail' (Gore Vidal)

'Success is the one unpardonable sin against one's fellows'
(Irving Berlin)

'Success is a public affair. Failure is a private funeral' (Rosalind
Russell)

Oh, to be in England – ten views of the English

'An Englishman, even if he is quite alone, forms an orderly queue of one' (George Mikes)

'The English instinctively admire any man who has no talent and is modest about it' (James Agee)

'The English find ill-health not only interesting but respectable, and often experience death in the effort to avoid a fuss' (Pamela Frankau)

'One of the freedoms of the English is the freedom from culture' (Lord Goodman)

'Englishmen know instinctively that whatever the world needs most is whatever is best for Great Britain' (Ogden Nash)

'The English may not like music, but they absolutely love the noise it makes' (Sir Thomas Beecham)

'When two Englishmen meet their first talk is of the weather' (Samuel Johnson)

'The English never forgive a man for being clever' (Lord Hailsham)

'The English have an extraordinary ability for flying into a great calm' (Alexander Woollcott)

'The English never smash in a face. They merely refrain from asking it to dinner' (Margaret Halsey)

The things they say – ten more bitchy put-downs

Donny Osmond: 'He has Van Gogh's ear for music' (Orson Welles)

Ronald Reagan: 'A triumph of the embalmer's art' (Gore Vidal)

Frank Sinatra: 'He's the kind of guy that, when he dies, he's going up to heaven and give God a bad time for making him bald' (Marlon Brando)

Jimmy Carter: 'I don't know what people have got against him; he's done nothing' (Bob Hope)

Jack Kerouac: 'That's not writing – that's typing' (Truman Capote)

Woody Allen: 'He has a face that convinces you that God is a cartoonist' (Jack Kroll)

Tony Benn: 'He immatures with age' (Harold Wilson)

Marilyn Monroe: 'A vacuum with nipples' (Otto Preminger)

Muhammad Ali: 'He stings like a bee but lives like a WASP' (Eamonn Andrews)

Richard Nixon: 'He is a man that had the morals of a private detective' (William Burroughs)

Music

Are you a declining pop star? Ten tell-tale signs

Your latest single peaks at number 87 in the charts
You release a 'Greatest Hits' album and nobody recognises the songs
Your last appearance was on *Give Us A Clue*
Your next appearance is in magistrates' court
You announce that you're 'going back to your roots'
Your revival tour is cancelled due to lack of interest
You sign up to do a rock opera of *Macbeth*
You become born again
You do a season in pantomime
You appear in an advertising campaign for electric showers

They don't write 'em like this any more – ten song titles to savour

Don't Be Cruel To A Vegetabuel (Leslie Sarony, 1929)
When The Breath Bids Your Girlfriend's Body Goodbye (Johnny Temple, 1938)
Dance Of The Doinks (Spud Murphy Orchestra, 1939)
This Is The Way The Puff Puff Goes (Rhythmic Eight, 1928)
Bald-Headed Mama (Billy Banks, 1932)
Rasputin, That High-Falutin' Lovin' Man (The Three Keys, 1933)
Abercrombie Had A Zombie (Fats Waller, 1940)
Little Willie Blues (Jabbo Smith, 1929)
Bennie The Bumble Bee Feels Bum (Dixieland Swingstars, 1937)
Cock-A-Doodle I'm Off My Noodle (Hooley Ahola's Vikings, 1926)

Ten classic singles which didn't make the top ten

Light My Fire: The Doors (Number 49 in 1967)
Candle In The Wind: Elton John (Number 11 in 1974)
California Girls: The Beach Boys (Number 26 in 1965)
Tutti Frutti: Little Richard (Number 29 in 1957)
California Dreamin': The Mamas and the Papas (Number 23 in 1966)
Hi-Ho Silver Lining: Jeff Beck (Number 14 in 1967)
Roxanne: The Police (Number 12 in 1979)
The First Time Ever I Saw Your Face: Roberta Flack (Number 14 in 1972)
Young Americans: David Bowie (Number 18 in 1975)
How Long: Ace (Number 20 in 1974)

Underground music – a tube travellers' top ten

Waterloo (Abba)
London Bridge (Bread)
Baker Street (Gerry Rafferty)
Victoria (The Kinks)
Angel of the Morning (P. P. Arnold)
Sunny Goodge Street (Donovan)
Good Old Arsenal (Arsenal FC)
Straight to the Bank (Bill Summers)
Bond Street (Burt Bacharach)
Finchley Central (New Vaudeville Band)

Write your own rap – ten phrases you'll need

Turn up the bass
Get up
Get down
Pump it up
Heat it up

Get pumping
Get thumping
Do it
Hit the beat
Shake your thing

Ten surprising opera buffs

Eric Clapton
Derek Jameson
Elvis Costello
Bruce Oldfield
Eartha Kitt

Mike Smith
Freddie Mercury
Anita Dobson
Lulu
Michael Fish

'I'll just put you on hold' – the top ten telephone muzak tracks

The Four Seasons (Vivaldi)
Moonshadow (The Shadows)
Eine Kleine Nachtmusik (Mozart)
Sing (The Carpenters)
Brandenburg Concertos (Bach)
Ballad For Adeline (Richard Clayderman)
Water Music (Handel)
Hello (Lionel Richie)
Nutcracker Suite (Tchaikovsky)
Why Worry (Dire Straits)

Ten repetitive hits

Money Money Money (Abba)
Girls Girls Girls (Sailor)
Yummy Yummy Yummy (Ohio Express)
Fun Fun Fun (The Beach Boys)
Turn! Turn! Turn! (The Byrds)
Stop Stop Stop (The Hollies)
Shame Shame Shame (Shirley and Company)
Hi Hi Hi (Paul McCartney)
Jeannie Jeannie Jeannie (Eddie Cochran)
Alright Alright Alright (Mungo Jerry)

A family tree of rock groups

Sister Sledge
Brother Beyond
Big Daddy
The Mothers of Invention
The Mamas and the Papas

The Thompson Twins
Son of Man
Our Daughter's Wedding
Our Kid
Family

Ten people who had posthumous hit records

Elvis Presley: *It's Only Love* (1980, Number 3)
Jim Reeves: *Distant Drums* (1966, Number 1)
Jackie Wilson: *Reet Petite* (1986, Number 1)
John Lennon: *Woman* (1981, Number 1)
Jimi Hendrix: *Voodoo Chile* (1970, Number 1)
Buddy Holly: *It Doesn't Matter Anymore* (1959, Number 1)
Laurel and Hardy: *The Trail of the Lonesome Pine* (1975, Number 2)
Eddie Cochran: *Three Steps to Heaven* (1960, Number 1)
Otis Redding: *The Dock of the Bay* (1968, Number 3)
Bob Marley: *Buffalo Soldier* (1983, Number 4)

The first ten songs on Top of the Pops

I Only Want to Be with You (Dusty Springfield)
I Wanna Be Your Man (The Rolling Stones)
Glad All Over (The Dave Clark Five)
Stay (The Hollies)
Hippy Hippy Shake (The Swinging Blue Jeans)
Don't Talk to Him (Cliff Richard and the Shadows)
You were Made for Me (Freddie and the Dreamers)
24 Hours from Tulsa (Gene Pitney)
She Loves You (The Beatles)
I Wanna Hold Your Hand (The Beatles)

Ten pop remakes that became Number One in the charts

A Groovy Kind of Love: Phil Collins, 1988 (originally by the Mindbenders)

With a Little Help from My Friends: Wet Wet Wet, 1988 (The Beatles)

La Bamba: Los Lobos, 1987 (Ritchie Valens)

Everything I Own: Boy George, 1987 (Bread)

Caravan of Love: The Housemartins, 1986 (Isley Jasper Isley)

Don't Leave Me This Way: Communards, 1986 (Harold Melvin and the Bluenotes)

Living Doll: Cliff Richard and the Young Ones, 1986 (Cliff Richard)

Dancing in the Street: David Bowie and Mick Jagger, 1985 (Martha Reeves and the Vandellas)

I Got You Babe: UB40 with Chrissie Hynde, 1985 (Sonny and Cher)

Spirit in the Sky: Doctor and the Medics, 1986 (Norman Greenbaum)

The ten most covered Beatles songs

Yesterday
Something
Hey Jude
Fool on the Hill
Eleanor Rigby
The Long and Winding Road
Michelle
With a Little Help from My Friends
Day Tripper
Let It Be

'Any colour, as long as it's blue . . .' Ten Elvis numbers

Blue Guitar
Blue Hawaii
Blue Moon
Blue River
Blue Christmas

Blue Eyes Crying in the Rain
Blue Moon of Kentucky
Blue Suede Shoes
Indescribably Blue
Moody Blue

Together at last! Ten pop partnerships waiting to happen

Donna Summer and Johnny Winter
Gregory Abbott and Elvis Costello
Gladys Knight and Doris Day
Kate Bush and Robert Plant
Percy Sledge and Phoebe Snow
Mike Batt and Kenny Ball
Barry White and Cilla Black
Eddie Rabbitt and Willie Hutch
Samantha Fox and Marsha Hunt
Eric Carmen and the Bay City Rollers

Around the world in ten songs

The Lebanon (Human League)
Vietnam (Jimmy Cliff)
Cambodia (Kim Wilde)
Israel (Siouxsie and the Banshees)
America (Simon and Garfunkel)
Mexico (Long John Baldry)
Brazil (Crispy and Company)
Africa (Toto)
Panama (Van Halen)
Bangla Desh (George Harrison)

Take one – original working titles of ten Beatles songs

Miss Daisy Hawkins (*Eleanor Rigby*)
Hello Hello (*Hello, Goodbye*)
Aerial Tour Instrumental (*Flying*)
In the Life of (*Day in the Life*)
Scrambled Eggs (*Yesterday*)
Granny Smith (*Love You To*)
Seventeen (*I Saw Her Standing There*)
Mark I (*Tomorrow Never Knows*)
Won't Be There with You (*Think for Yourself*)
Laxton's Superb (*I Want to Tell You*)

Now we're all green – a vegetarian top ten

Little Red Courgette
Blue Swede Shoes
And The Beet Goes On
Peas Please Me
Lettuce Be
Aubergine Genie
Will You Still Love Me To Marrow?
Who's Sorrel Now?
'Cos I Love You
Twist And Sprout

Ten members of the musical nobility

Prince
Queen
King Crimson
Duke Ellington
Count Basie

Earl Hines
The Barron Knights
Nat King Cole
Sir Charles Thompson
Screaming Lord Sutch

The first ten records played on Radio 1

Flowers in the Rain (The Move)
Massachusetts (The Bee Gees)
Even the Bad Times are Good (The Tremeloes)
Fakin' It (Simon and Garfunkel)
The Day I Met Marie (Cliff Richard)
You Can't Hurry Love (The Supremes)
The Last Waltz (Engelbert Humperdinck)
Baby Now that I've Found You (The Foundations)
Good Times (Eric Burdon and the Animals)
A Banda (Herb Alpert and the Tijuana Brass)

'Hope I die before I get old . . .'
Ten rock stars who did

Brian Jones, 27 (drowned)
Marc Bolan, 29 (car crash)
Sam Cooke, 29 (shot)
Buddy Holly, 22 (plane crash)
Sid Vicious, 21 (drugs overdose)
Otis Redding, 26 (plane crash)
Paul Kossoff, 25 (heart failure)
Eddie Cochran, 21 (car crash)
Duane Allman, 24 (motorcycle crash)
Janis Joplin, 27 (drugs overdose)

A calendar of songs

January (Pilot)
January February (Barbara Dickson)
March of the Mods (Joe Loss)
April Come She Will (Simon and Garfunkel)
May Each Day (Andy Williams)
June Is Bustin' Out All Over (Gordon Macrae)
Fourth of July (John Christie)
August (Love)
September (Earth, Wind and Fire)
October (U2)
November 22nd 1963 (Destroy All Monsters)
December '63 – Oh What a Night (The Four Seasons)

Now starring in a song near you – ten actors immortalised in pop

Bette Davis Eyes (Kim Carnes)
Robert De Niro's Waiting (Bananarama)
He Looks like Spencer Tracy Now (Deacon Blue)
Michael Caine (Madness)
Hey Bogart (Nik Kershaw)
Errol Flynn (Dogs D'Amour)
The Ballad of Me and Shirley Maclaine (Danny Wilson)
Marlon Brando (Elton John)
John Wayne is Big Leggy (Haysi Fantayzee)
James Dean (The Eagles)

We thought they were so hip – ten albums you should now hide

Concerto for Group and Orchestra (Deep Purple)
Birds of Fire (Mahavishnu Orchestra)
Five Bridges (Nice)
Pictures at an Exhibition (Emerson, Lake and Palmer)
The Six Wives of Henry VIII (Rick Wakeman)
A Gift from a Flower to a Garden (Donovan)
Phaedra (Tangerine Dream)
Oxygene (Jean-Michel Jarre)
In the Court of the Crimson King (King Crimson)
In-A-Gadda-Da-Vida (Iron Butterfly)

Ten songs for ageing rockers

Hit Me with Your Walking Stick
We're All Going on a Saga Holiday
Blue Suede Slippers
Saturday Night's Alright for Bingo
The Grandkids are Alright
Nights in White Winceyette
Now I'm Sixty-Four
Magic Bus Pass
Blue Rinse for a Blue Day
Concessionary Ticket to Ride

Rock 'n' roll-mop: a fishmonger's top ten

Guppy love (Donny Osmond)
Mussels (Diana Ross)
Can you fillet (The Jacksons)
The moray see you (Chris Montez)
Carp wash (Rose Royce)
Never mind the pollocks (The Sex Pistols)
Ain't no stoppin huss now (McFadden and Whitehead)
Hake rattle and roll (Bill Haley)
Prawn to run (Bruce Springsteen)
Salmon to watch over me (Sting)

The Media

Who says TV is getting worse? The first ten programmes shown by the BBC

Opening of the BBC Television Service in November, 1936, by Postmaster-General Major the Right Honourable G. C. Tryon, and Chairman of the BBC, Mr R. C. Norman

British Movietone News

Variety, featuring Adele Dixon, Buck & Bubbles and The Lai Founs Chinese Jugglers

Television Comes to London, 'an insight into production routine'

Picture Page, a magazine of topical interest with Joan Miller as 'The Switchboard Girl'

Alsatians, a display by champion Alsatians from the Metropolitan and Essex Society's Show

The Golden Hind, a model of Drake's famous ship made by L. A. Stock, 'a bus driver who describes its construction'

Starlight, with Bebe Daniels and Ben Lyon, 'the Hollywood Film Stars'

Starlight, with Manuela Del Rio in Spanish dances, accompanied by piano and guitar

Martin Taubman and his Electronde, a demonstration of its music and effects

The longest-running programmes on television

Come Dancing (1950)

The Sooty Show (1952)

Panorama (1953)

This Is Your Life (1953)

This Week (1956)

What the Papers Say (1956)

The Sky at Night (1957)

Grandstand (1958)

Blue Peter (1958)

Coronation Street (1960)

They made their excuses and left – ten former journalists

Benito Mussolini

Dennis Potter

Burgess Meredith

Barbara Taylor Bradford

Steve Harley

Patti Smith

Ali MacGraw

Frederick Forsyth

Mark Knopfler

Tom Stoppard

'What's on the other side?' The first ten programmes shown on ITV

Opening Ceremony from the Guildhall (22 September, 1955)

Channel Nine, a 'sparkling' variety show with Jack Jackson, Hughie Green, Billy Cotton and Harry Secombe

Drama – Robert Morley introduces excerpts from *The Importance of Being Earnest*, *Baker's Dozen* and *Private Lives*

Professional Boxing from Shoreditch (Terence Murphy *v* Lew Lazar)

News and newsreel

Gala Night at The Mayfair with Leslie Mitchell

Star Cabaret with Billy Ternant and His Orchestra

Preview of programmes to be shown 'in the coming months'

Sixpenny Corner, soap opera about 'Young Bill and Sally Norton and their garage at Sixpenny Corner in rural Springwood'

Hands About The House, advice on 'practical tasks – the sort usually left to husbands – such as wallpapering, simple repairs, et cetera. Today, Elsa Court shows how to make a frame for flowers'

Women's magazine-speak: a guide to interpretation

Gourmet cooking on a budget: Sausages with peculiar fillings
Practical fitness programme: Running up and down stairs
Be your own boss: Rent a knitting machine
A new you for the 1990s: Lipstick special offer
Break out!: Have a weekend in Guernsey
Financial advice: How to open a bank account
Colourful cookery: Saffron with everything
Try our personality test: Just in case you thought there was
     nothing wrong with you
Handy hints: Don't throw those empty yoghurt pots away
Improved self-image: Better sex life

So you want to be a newsreader – ten things you must be able to do

Pronounce 'Uranus' without giggling
Pretend to have a conversation with your co-presenter at the
     end of the broadcast
Smile inanely when introducing an item about the Royal
     Family
Shuffle blank papers meaningfully
Pronounce 'guerrilla' as 'gerr-ia'
Make guest appearances on comedy shows
Say names like 'Tadeusz Mazowiecki' without spitting
Evince an air of concern about the outcome of local elections
     in Ulan Bator
Make excruciating puns after stories about ducks that can sing
     the national anthem
Wear shoes, even though nobody can see your feet

Launch a rival to Today – ten articles you'll need

What your choice of coffee says about you and your partner
Going green: how TV commercials are facing up to the challenge
Are you in love with your boss?
The eyes have it! How glasses can make or break your relationship
Are you and your partner environmentally compatible?
Play together and stay together: working it out in the gym
The *real* life of Fred the Flourgrader
Coat and car: how the woman in the VW ad could have it both ways
Does work interfere with sex in the office?
How portable phones make it easier for him to cheat on you

TV previews: a guide to interpretation

Offbeat sitcom: No sofa
Classic sitcom: Repeat
Regional programme: Time to make the tea
Special opera performance: Franchise up for renewal
Celebrity panel: Contains an astrologer and a 1960s actress
Star-studded variety: Bonnie Langford tops the bill
Unmissable cameo performance: Sir John Gielgud
Mini-series: Twelve hours of missable cameo performances
Based on a bestseller: The author wouldn't recognise it
True-life drama: Roger Cook gets punched

Ten new characters for Viz

Halitosis Henry – Take His Breath Away!
Billy Bore – He Knows Every Fact In The World!
Roger The Miserable Old Codger
Doreen Dandruff
Wiggy Willie – He Can't Keep His Hair On!
The Zit Squad – They Always Hit The Spot!
Walter And His Talking Wheelie Bin – They're Both Full Of
  Rubbish!
Mincing MacDonald, Gay Chief Of The Clans
Barbara And Her Expanding Bra – They Go Too Far!
Pompous Patrick Perfect – What a Prat!

Ten ways to get your letter read out on Points of View

Write the word 'very' at least twenty-five times
Add a PS commenting on Anne Robinson's hairstyle
Refer to BBC management as 'them upstairs'
Use green ink
Beg to see an excerpt from a natural history programme
Say you're fed up with people criticising the BBC
If you're a woman, ask for more sport on TV
If you're a man, ask for less sport on TV
Use lots of exclamation marks!
Pretend you have a 'funny' address, like Pratt's Bottom

Ten classic headlines

Police Discover Crack in Australia
Drunk gets Nine Months in Violin Case
Milk Drinkers are Turning to Powder
Deaf Mute gets New Hearing in Killing
Stiff Opposition Expected to Casketless Funeral Plan
Convict Escapes Noose: Jury Hung
Complaints about Referees Growing Ugly
Defendant's Speech Ends in Long Sentence
Caribbean Islands Drift to Left
Dr Ruth to Talk about Sex with Newspaper Editors

Ten programmes to pep up the TV schedules

Suddenly It's Ian McCaskill!
Floyd on Flatulence
Jimmy Tarbuck's Antique Joke Show
Chris Tarrant Presents . . . the Clips that Clive James Didn't
The M25 Roadshow
Pro-Celebrity Knitting (Sky TV only)
Muriel Gray Says 'Come On Down!'
Comedy Classics: The Best of National Weather
The Crumpled Clothes Show with Patrick Moore
Def and Daft II

Ten holidays for Wish You Were Here . . . ? to investigate

The 'Last Days of America/World Cup 94' Combined
Package
The Pamella Bordes Activity Weekend
The Budget Self-Catering Airport Lounge Break
The Four-Star Self-Catering Airport Lounge Break (includes
seat)
The Stay-at-Home Supersaver
'A Taste of Scunthorpe'
The Salman Rushdie Mystery Tour
The John Hurt Heritage Crawl
'Syd and Eddie's Historic Manchester'
The BritRail Family Awayday Off-Peak Poundstretcher
Bargain Rover (only available after 9.43 a.m. on
alternate Thursdays when there's an 'r' in the month)

Prime time marriages – ten TV couples

Mike Smith and Sarah Greene
Keith Chegwin and Maggie Philbin
Paul Heiney and Libby Purves
John Stapleton and Lynn Faulds-Wood
Richard Madeley and Judy Finnigan
Michael Parkinson and Mary Parkinson
Desmond Wilcox and Esther Rantzen
Cliff Michelmore and Jean Metcalfe
Robin Ray and Susan Stranks
Bernard Braden and Barbara Kelly

Journolists: an editorial charter for the 1990s

We will not mention Kenneth Branagh, even when it's in the public interest

All mistakes will be promptly blamed on somebody else

Right of reply will be granted if deemed appropriate, i.e. on receipt of a large amount of used £5 notes

We will not intrude into personal grief (e.g. Fergie's dress sense)

Information will be gathered by straightforward means – it will be entirely made up

Readers' complaints will be referred to an omnibusman (there'll be one along in a minute)

Unfair references to weight, hairstyle, size of nose, et cetera, will continue to be made

A readers' panel will be created by the finest craftsmen we can find

Race, colour and creed – yes, we're in favour of them

Anyone who takes us to the Press Council will be crossed off our Christmas card list

For the Record

Ten unconsummated marriages

Jean Harlow and Paul Bern
Marie Stopes and Reginald Ruggles Gate
Rudolph Valentino and Jean Acker
Sammy Davis Jnr and Loray White
Stanley Spencer and Patricia Preece
Eva Bartok and William Wordsworth
Henry VIII and Anne of Cleves
George Bernard Shaw and Charlotte Townsend
John Ruskin and Effie Gray
Chi-Chi and An-An

The first ten subjects of This Is Your Life (starting 1955)

Eamonn Andrews
Yvonne Bailey (French Resistance heroine)
Ted Ray
Reverend James Butterworth (worked with underprivileged
     children)
C. B. Fry
Johanna Harris (British Red Cross)
Donald Campbell
Joe Brannelly (music publisher)
Stanley Matthews
Henry Starling (porter at Billingsgate Market)

The first ten subjects on ITV's This Is Your Life *(starting 1969)*

Des O'Connor
Bobby Charlton
Harry Driver
Twiggy
Honor Blackman

The Beverley Sisters
John Fairfax
Henry Cooper
Jackie Stewart
Jimmy Savile

Ten of the oddest luxury items chosen on Desert Island Discs

The Mona Lisa (Arthur Scargill)
The Albert Memorial (Hermione Gingold)
A stick of marijuana (Norman Mailer)
A revolver (Artur Rubenstein)
A television set which doesn't work (Sir Robert Mark)
The Koh-i-Noor diamond (Stefan Grapelli)
A replica of Broadcasting House (Sir Harry Secombe)
All his own films (Otto Preminger)
One million pounds in £1 notes (Eric Robinson)
A plastic inflatable woman (Gary Glitter)

The Dave Allen factor – ten people who have used the 'F' word on TV

Johnny Rotten
Kenneth Tynan
Peregrine Worsthorne
Anthony Burgess
Bob Geldof

Jools Holland
Dustin Hoffman
Elvis Costello
Steven Berkoff
Eric Clapton

Ten of this year's lesser-known anniversaries

Traffic wardens took to the streets of Britain 30 years ago
The electric chair was first used in America 100 years ago
The first air raid on Britain took place 75 years ago when
bombs were dropped on Norfolk from a Zeppelin
Leon Trotsky was murdered with an ice-pick 50 years ago
Brasilia became the capital of Brazil 30 years ago
The first branch of the Women's Institute opened 75 years
ago
The dental drill was invented 200 years ago in New York
Budgies first came to Britain from Australia 150 years ago
Rubber wellingtons were introduced 125 years ago by the
North British Rubber Company of Edinburgh
Nylon stockings went on sale in America 50 years ago

Ten initials – the other ones

BMA (British Majorettes Association)
RSC (Royal Society of Canada)
CIA (Chemical Industries Association)
IMF (International Metalworkers Federation)
EEC (Eurocontrol Experimental Centre)
FA (Faculty of Actuaries)
IBA (International Bar Association)
CID (Council of Industrial Design)
ICC (International Christian Committee)
STD (Doctor of Sacred Theology)

Ten people who took their mother's surname

Pablo Picasso (father's name Ruiz)
Marilyn Monroe (father's name Mortensen)
Leslie Howard (father's name Stainer)
Rita Hayworth (father's name Cansino)
Patti Davis (daughter of Nancy Davis and Ronald Reagan)
Simone Signoret (father's name Kaminker)
Gloria Grahame (father's name Hallward)
Shelley Winters (father's name Schrift)
Shirley Maclaine (father's name Beaty)
Jean Harlow (father's name Carpenter)

'And in the silver medal position . . .' Ten of history's second places

Second pope: St Linus (67–79AD)
Second woman Prime Minister: Indira Gandhi (elected 1966)
Second test-tube baby: Alistair Montgomery (born 1979)
Second sub-four-minute miler: John Landy (1954)
Second man on the moon: Edwin Aldrin (1969)
Second team to climb Mount Everest: Ernest Reiss and Fritz
      Luchsinger (1956)
Second circumnavigation of the globe: Francis Drake (1577–
      80)
Second expedition to reach the South Pole: Captain Robert
      Scott's (1911)
Second leader of the Capone gang: Frank ('The Enforcer')
      Nitti (killed himself 1943)
Second person to win £1m in Britain: Irene Dunn (in a
      newspaper game 1985)

The world's ten most expensive paintings

'Portrait of Dr Gachet' by **Van Gogh** sold to Mr Ryoei Saito
of Japan for £49.1m in 1990

'Au Moulin de la Galette' by **Renoir** sold to Mr Ryoei Saito
of Japan for £45m in 1990

'Irises' by **Van Gogh** sold to Alan Bond for £30.2m in 1987

'Yo Picasso' by **Picasso** sold to an anonymous buyer for £27m
in 1989

'Sunflowers' by **Van Gogh** sold to Yasuda Fire and Marine
Insurance for £24.75m in 1987

'Young Acrobat and Harlequin' by **Picasso** sold to the
Japanese store Mitsukoshi for £20.9m in 1988

'Dans La Prairie' by **Monet** sold to an anonymous buyer for
£14.3m in 1988

'Mata Mua' by **Gauguin** sold to Baron Thyssen-Bornemisza
for £13.7m in 1989

'Maternité' by **Picasso** sold to an unknown South American
buyer for £13.2m in 1988

'Le Pont de Trinquetaille' by **Van Gogh** sold to an
anonymous buyer for £12.65m in 1987

Ten countries we've fought wars against

Holland	Turkey
China	Egypt
Austria	Denmark
America	Hungary
Sweden	North Korea

Ten men who are forty this year

Noddy Holder
David Cassidy
William Hurt
Peter Gabriel
Phil Parkes

Stevie Wonder
Charlie George
Simon Cadell
Malcolm Macdonald
Matthew Kelly

Ten women who are forty this year

The Princess Royal
Susan George
Julie Walters
Mary Hopkin
Suzi Quatro

Gemma Craven
Sissy Spacek
Joan Armatrading
Morgan Fairchild
Liza Goddard

Those who would be Wogan – ten people who have stood in for Terry

Joanna Lumley
Ronnie Corbett
Felicity Kendall
Ben Elton
Anna Ford

Bruce Forsyth
Sue Lawley
David Frost
Selina Scott
Jonathan Ross

Ten Rolls-Royce owners

Vladimir Lenin
Mao Tse-Tung
Idi Amin
Lawrence of Arabia
Grigori Rasputin

Benito Mussolini
Leonid Brezhnev
Ayatollah Khomeini
George Bernard Shaw
Mikhail Gorbachev

Ten actors who have appeared in Coronation Street

Ben Kingsley
Prunella Scales
Gorden Kaye
Joanna Lumley
Michael Ball

Martin Shaw
Michael Elphick
Paul Shane
Mollie Sugden
Kathy Staff

'Ello, 'ello, 'ello – ten former policemen

Christopher Dean
Ray Reardon
John Arlott
Geoff Capes
Roy Clarke

Errol Flynn
Josef Locke
George Orwell
Aldo Ray
Gilbert Harding

I was a teenage bride – ten girls who married young

Loretta Lynn, 13
Zsa Zsa Gabor, 15
Emma Ridley, 15
Regine, 16
Eva Bartok, 15
Myra Gale Brown (Mrs Jerry Lee Lewis), 13
Marilyn Monroe, 16
Barbara Kelly, 17
Gloria Swanson, 17
Annie Oakley, 15

Ten children of clergymen

Grace Jones
Fiona Richmond
John Hurt
Virginia Wade
John Wells

David Frost
Ingmar Bergman
David Steel
Andrew Faulds
Alice Cooper

Ten of the oddest items sold at auction

George Washington's laundry bill, dated 1787 ($1100 in 1976)
London Bridge (£1.2m in 1968)
180,000 dead cats (£3 15s a ton in 1890)
Judy Garland's false eyelashes ($125 in 1979)
The first photograph of a photographer taking a photograph (£5000 in 1977)
Napoleon's penis (£2000 in 1977)
Maori chief's head ($20,400 in 1977)
Davy Crockett's hat ($10,000 in 1938)
Anne of Austria's chastity belt (£650 in 1912)
A flush toilet made by Thomas Crapper ($1400 in 1914)

It's never too late – ten older fathers

Telly Savalas (at 60)
John Mortimer (at 61)
Charlie Chaplin (at 73)
Arthur English (at 61)
Pablo Picasso (at 62)

Cary Grant (at 62)
Marlon Brando (at 65)
Denis Compton (at 66)
Yves Montand (at 67)
Andrés Segovia (at 77)

WWII special – ten other things which happened the year war broke out

Teflon was patented
Darts were banned in Glasgow pubs for being 'too dangerous'
The first Citizens Advice Bureau was opened
The disposable aerosol spray can was invented
The last public guillotining took place in France
Portsmouth won the FA Cup
The first jet plane made its maiden flight
The Committee on Nursing Services reported that 'Nurses are
    overworked and underpaid'
King George VI became the first British monarch to visit the
    US
Sigmund Freud died

Ten people who were adopted

Debbie Harry
Henry Morton Stanley
Gerald Ford
Fatima Whitbread
Jeanette Winterson

Phillip Whitehead
Kiri Te Kanawa
James Michener
George Cole
Edgar Wallace

Ten couples who were born on the same day

Princess Diana and Carl Lewis (1 July 1961)
Yoko Ono and Bobby Robson (18 February 1933)
Willie Rushton and Robert Redford (18 August 1937)
Glenda Jackson and Albert Finney (9 May 1936)
Margaret Thatcher and Lenny Bruce (13 October 1925)
The Bishop of Durham and Paul Newman (26 January 1925)
Michael Jackson and Lenny Henry (29 August 1958)
Maureen Lipman and Donovan (10 May 1946)
Dickie Bird and Jayne Mansfield (19 April 1933)
Prince Andrew and Lesley Ash (19 February 1960)

Ten university drop-outs

Michael Douglas	Jane Fonda
Mick Jagger	Warren Beatty
Burt Lancaster	Bernardo Bertolucci
Carly Simon	Richard Dreyfuss
Bill Cosby	Candice Bergen

Old school ties – ten couples who share an Alma Mater

Richard Branson and Peregrine Worsthorne (Stowe)
Peter Gabriel and Lord Rees-Mogg (Charterhouse)
Claire Rayner and Elizabeth Emanuel (City of London Girls')
Michael Foot and Sir David Lean (Leighton Park)
Denis Healey and Mollie Sugden (Drake and Tonsons'
        Kindergarten)
Nigel Lawson and Andrew Lloyd-Webber (Westminster)
Captain Mark Phillips and Chris de Burgh (Marlborough)
Lynda Chalker and Sarah Miles (Roedean)
Salman Rushdie and Tom King (Rugby)
Tony Blackburn and Gareth Edwards (Millfield)

What ten people did at the age of sixteen

John Lennon got his first guitar and formed The Quarry Men
Lesley-Anne Down won the title 'Prettiest teenager in
    England'
Richard Branson left school to start a magazine called *Student*
Tracey Ullman joined the Second Generation dance troupe
Billy Graham had the religious experience which led to his
    conversion
Jackie Collins was expelled from school for smoking
Margot Fonteyn danced Odette in *Swan Lake*
David Puttnam started as a messenger boy in an advertising
    agency
Shirley Bassey left home to work in a factory wrapping
    chamber pots
Mozart wrote eight symphonies and an opera

Nice work – ten classical musicians who can earn over £10,000 a night

André Previn
Daniel Barenboim
Mstislav Rostropovich
Kiri Te Kanawa
Luciano Pavarotti

Placido Domingo
Vladimir Ashkenazy
Jessye Norman
Pinchas Zuckerman
Leonard Bernstein

Ten World War II pilots

George Bush
Hughie Green
James Stewart
Ian Smith
Raymond Baxter

Sir Hector Monro
Kenneth Wolstenholme
Sir Rex Hunt
Ted Croker
Bill Edrich

To boldly go . . . ten countries which have had men in space

Poland

France

East Germany

Hungary

Cuba

Romania

Vietnam

Czechoslovakia

Bulgaria

India

Ten men who were prisoners-of-war

Sir Laurens van der Post

Clive Dunn

The Earl of Harewood

Sam Kydd

Roy Dotrice

Robert Kee

Dixie Dean

Russell Braddon

Angus Maude

Ronald Searle

The first ten castaways on Desert Island Discs *(starting January, 1942)*

Vic Oliver (comedian)

James Agate (critic)

Commander Campbell (mariner and explorer)

C. B. Cochran (showman)

Pat Kirkwood (actress)

Jack Hylton (bandleader)

Captain A. E. Dingle (explorer)

Joan Jay (glamour girl)

Canon W. H. Elliott (precentor of the Chapels Royal)

Arthur Askey (comedian)

Ten couples who married each other twice

Don Johnson and Melanie Griffith
Dionne Warwick and Bill Elliott
Natalie Wood and Robert Wagner
Elizabeth Taylor and Richard Burton
Dorothy Parker and Alan Campbell
Paul Hogan and Noelene Edwards
Elliot Gould and Jenny Bogart
Jane Wyman and Fred Karger
A. J. Ayer and Dee Wells
Sarah Miles and Robert Bolt

Ten lesser-known patron saints

St Barthelemy (coconut pickers)
St Bernadino of Siena (public relations)
St Genesius (shorthand-typists)
St Paula (beards)
St Jude (lost causes)
St Gabriel (TV workers)
St Vitus (comedians)
St Appollonia (dentists)
St Gallen (avalanches)
St Ethelric (optimists)

Ten people who have adopted children

Bob Monkhouse
David Bellamy
Penelope Keith
David Steel
Colin Welland

Mia Farrow
Burt Reynolds
Joan Lestor
Julie Andrews
Ilie Nastase

Money, money, money – the ten highest prices for pop memorabilia at auction

John Lennon's hand-decorated Rolls Royce Phantom V (£1,768,000 in 1985 at Sotheby's)

John Lennon's Mercedes Benz (£125,000 in 1989 at Christie's)

Elvis Presley's Phantom V limousine (£110,000 in 1986 at Sotheby's)

An unreleased film of the Beatles in America in 1965 (£26,000 in 1986 at Christie's)

Elvis Presley's white stage suit (£26,000 in 1988 at Phillips)

A two-hour taped interview with John Lennon made in 1968 by two university students (£23,650 in 1987 at Sotheby's)

Collection of thirty-four Peter Max posters, including an unpublished Bob Dylan poster (£21,290 in 1989 at Sotheby's)

Biographical booklet, *The Beatles From Apple*, annotated by John Lennon (£20,950 in 1986 at Sotheby's)

John Lennon manuscript for an unpublished book (£17,600 in 1984 at Sotheby's)

Elton John's 1940s Wurlitzer jukebox (£17,600 in 1988 at Sotheby's)

Ten people who began their careers as secretaries

The Duchess of York
Soraya Khashoggi
Anneka Rice
Sophie Mirman
Lady Elspeth Howe

Su Pollard
Cilla Black
Lady Marcia Falkender
Samuel Beckett
Jan Leeming

'But I know what I don't like . . .' Ten art attacks

Bryan Organ's picture of the Princess of Wales in the National Portrait Gallery was slashed with a knife by an art student from Northern Ireland (1981)

The statue of Lady Godiva in Coventry was daubed with foothigh letters which said 'Women are angry, they will fight back' (1980)

The Little Mermaid in Copenhagen harbour was decapitated with a hacksaw as a 'protest against the decapitation of buildings' in Denmark (1964)

A Rubens portrait of King Philip IV of Spain was set on fire in a Zurich museum by a German protesting against 'pollution of the environment' (1985)

Da Vinci's cartoon, The Virgin and Child with St Anne and St John, at the National Gallery, was peppered with shotgun pellets by a former soldier (1987)

A glass fibre woman in black underwear by the pop artist Allen Jones had acid thrown over it by two women to mark International Women's Day (1986)

Ten seventeenth-century Dutch masterpieces in an Amsterdam museum were knife slashed by a Dutchman protesting against the loss of his job (1989)

A painting by American artist Jo Baer was covered in lipstick kisses to 'cheer it up' when on loan to the Oxford Museum of Modern Art (1977)

Eight eighteenth-century statues of Greek gods at the Glasgow School of Art had their private parts chopped off by an unknown assailant (1987)

A Dutch artist slashed two diagonal cuts into a Vincent Van Gogh self-portrait in Amsterdam (1978)

What the famous collect

Judi Dench: dolls' houses and dolls' furniture
Edward Heath: Japanese prints
Siân Phillips: old tapestries
Barry Humphries: rare first editions
Leslie Crowther: Victorian ceramic pot lids
Tom Stoppard: literary autographs
Ronnie Barker: saucy postcards
Martina Navratilova: art deco statuettes
Freddie Mercury: Japanese dolls and Japanese carp
Tim Rice: cricket books

Ten things which are cheaper today than ten years ago

Microwave oven (£269 in 1980, £159 today)
Video film (£45 in 1980, £9.99 today)
Disposable razor (8p in 1980, 7p today)
Scottish farmed salmon (£2 per lb in 1980, £1.80 today)
Pocket calculator (£9.95 in 1980, £6.95 today)
Monthly TV rental (£13.95 in 1980, £12.95 today)
Two-week holiday in Disneyworld (£500 upwards in 1980, £250 upwards today)
Stereo radio cassette (£110 in 1980, £70 today)
A ton of landed herring (£496 in 1980, £121 today)
Three-hour blank video tape (£10.95 in 1980, £2.99 today)

Ten people who became pensioners this year

Princess Margaret
Harry Carpenter
Richard Baker
Benny Hill
Shirley Williams

George Cole
Tony Benn
Alan Whicker
Gerald Durrell
Ernie Wise

Literature

Ten unputdownable book titles

Who's Who in Baton Twirling (Don Sartell)
A Toddler's Guide to the Rubber Industry (D. Lowe)
Anorexia Nervosa in Bulgarian Bees (Jeanne d'Arc)
The Great Pantyhose Craft Book (Ed and Stevie Baldwin)
The Joy of Chickens (Dennis Nolan)
Why Bring That Up? A Guide to Seasickness (Joseph Franklin
     Montague)
*The History and Romance of Elastic Webbing Since the Dawn of
     Time* (Clifford A. Richmond)
Nasal Maintenance: Nursing Your Nose Through Troubled Times
     (William Alan Stuart)
The Magic of Telephone Evangelism (Harold E. Metcalf)
Proceedings of the Second International Workshop on Nude Mice
     (University of Tokyo Press)

Ten updated novels

A Tale of Twinned Cities
Crime and Community Service
Motel du Lac
Alice in Disneyland
The Mortgage as Big as the Ritz
1994
Of Mice and Cabinet Ministers
Three Men in a BMW
The Loneliness of the Long Distance Lorry Driver
War and Peace Studies

Ten books which are supposed to change your life

Jonathan Livingstone Seagull
The Women's Room
Fear of Flying
Zen and the Art of Motorcycle Maintenance
The Dice Man
The Female Eunuch
The I-Ching
On the Road
Superwoman
The Feminine Mystique

Ten books which actually do change your life

The Highway Code
The Good Food Guide
The A–Z
Halliwell's Film Guide
The Reader's Digest Cookery Year
The F-Plan Diet
The Family Doctor
The Good Beer Guide
The Yellow Pages
The Satanic Verses (if your name is Salman)

Ten book titles from other authors

From Here to Eternity by James Jones (from Rudyard Kipling's *Gentlemen Rankers*)

Gone with the Wind by Margaret Mitchell (from Ernest Dowson's *Cynara*)

The Grapes of Wrath by John Steinbeck (from Julia Ward Howe's *The Battle Hymn of the American Republic*)

Tender is the Night by Scott Fitzgerald (from John Keats' *Ode to a Nightingale*)

The Moon's a Balloon by David Niven (from e. e. cummings' *& N &*)

Of Mice and Men by John Steinbeck (from Robert Burns' *To a Mouse*)

Now Voyager by Olive Higgins Prouty (from Walt Whitman's *Leaves of Grass*)

Paths of Glory by Humphrey Cobb (from Thomas Gray's *Elegy in a Country Churchyard*)

For Whom the Bell Tolls by Ernest Hemingway (from John Donne's *Devotions*)

A Confederacy of Dunces by John Kennedy Toole (from Jonathan Swift's *Thoughts on Various Subjects*)

Ten corners of P. G. Wodehouse's England

Lower Smattering-on-the-Wissel
Eggmarsh St John
Upton Snodsbury
Twing
Much Middlefold
Bottsford Mortimer
Lower Shagley
Brinkley-cum-Snodsfield-in-the-Marsh
Chuffnell Regis
Ditteredge

A literary top ten

One Day in the Life of Ivan Denisovich (Alexander
      Solzhenitsyn)
The Two Faces of January (Patricia Highsmith)
Three Men in a Boat (Jerome K. Jerome)
Four Beauties (H. E. Bates)
Five on Kirrin Island (Enid Blyton)
Six Characters in Search of an Author (Luigi Pirandello)
The Seven Pillars of Wisdom (T. E. Lawrence)
Eight Black Horses (Ed McBain)
Nine Tailors (Dorothy L. Sayers)
Ten Little Indians (Agatha Christie)

The books they never wrote . . .

How to Win Friends and Influence People (Salman Rushdie)
Far from the Madding Crowd (Tom Wolfe)
Gone with the Wind (Claire Francis)
Vile Bodies (Rosemary Conley)
The Diary of a Nobody (Melvyn Bragg)
Hard Times (Jackie Collins)
The Invisible Man (John Mortimer)
Some More of Me Poems (Ted Hughes)
Love Story (Fay Weldon)
Great Expectations (Jeffrey Archer)

Spot the author – ten pseudonyms used by writers

Paul French (Isaac Asimov)
Basil Seal (Julian Barnes)
Peter Anthony (Peter and Anthony Shaffer)
Claire Morgan (Patricia Highsmith)
Robert Markham (Kingsley Amis)
Edgar Box (Gore Vidal)
Roland Allen (Alan Ayckbourn)
Albert Haddock (A. P. Herbert)
John Luckless (Clifford Irving)
Matilda Excellent (Daniel Farson)

The ten authors whose books are borrowed most from libraries

Catherine Cookson
Dick Francis
Jeffrey Archer
Wilbur Smith
Jack Higgins

Barbara Taylor Bradford
Len Deighton
Danielle Steel
Harold Robbins
Barbara Cartland

Ten actors who had novels published

Joan Collins (*Prime Time*)
Dirk Bogarde (*West of Sunset*)
George Kennedy (*Murder on Location*)
David Niven (*Once Over Lightly*)
Robert Shaw (*The Man in the Glass Booth*)
Anthony Sher (*Middlepost*)
Simone Signoret (*Adieu Volodia*)
Leslie Caron (*Vengeance*)
Diane Cilento (*The Manipulator*)
Tony Curtis (*Kid Andrew Cody and Julie Sparrow*)

Ten books and their original titles

Portnoy's Complaint (Philip Roth): A Jewish Patient Begins
 His Analysis
Lady Chatterley's Lover (D. H. Lawrence): Tenderness
The Postman Always Rings Twice (James M. Cain): Bar B-Q
Frankenstein (Mary Shelley): Prometheus Unchained
War and Peace (Leo Tolstoy): All's Well that Ends Well
Of Mice and Men (John Steinbeck): Something that Happened
Catch 22 (Joseph Heller): Catch 18
Gone with the Wind (Margaret Mitchell): Ba! Ba! Black Sheep
Treasure Island (Robert Louis Stevenson): The Sea Cook
The Happy Hooker (Xaviera Hollander): Come and Go

Ten people who have had books dedicated to them

Kingsley Amis (*XX Poems* by Philip Larkin)
Philip Larkin (*Lucky Jim* by Kingsley Amis)
Robert Bolt (*Second Fiddle* by Mary Wesley)
Diana Mosley (*Vile Bodies* by Evelyn Waugh)
Christopher Isherwood (*Myra Breckinridge* by Gore Vidal)
Brigid Brophy (*The Good Apprentice* by Iris Murdoch)
Robert Conquest (*Hearing Secret Harmonies* by Anthony
 Powell)
William Thackeray (*Jane Eyre* by Charlotte Brontë)
Iris Murdoch (*The Sweets of Pimlico* by A. N. Wilson)
Ivy Compton-Burnett (*The Spoilt City* by Olivia Manning)

Politics

Government-speak: *a guide to interpretation*

A blip: Runaway inflation
Signs of prosperity: Standing room only on commuter trains
Enterprise zone: Area of unemployment
Under-consumption: Poverty
Rationalisation: Replacing the tea lady with a vending machine
Changing demographics: Time to re-draw the electoral boundaries
Consumer power: It's up to you lot
Consolidation: Standing still
Retrenchment: Going backwards
Common sense: Pay rises below inflation

Ten political dirty tricks

Installing brass carriage lamps outside Dennis Skinner's house
Kidnapping Norman Tebbit and taking him to a Ben Elton concert
Stealing the heels off Colin Moynihan's shoes
Applying for planning permission to dump nuclear waste in Finchley
Putting Superglue on Tony Benn's pipe
Infiltrating Denis Healey's eyebrows
Ron Brown
Reminding someone they were in the SDP
Being made Opposition spokesman for overseas development
Appointing anyone Secretary of State for Northern Ireland

Ten Labour MPs who went to public school

Geoffrey Robinson (Emanuel School)
Greville Janner (St Paul's)
Tony Benn (Westminster)
Tam Dalyell (Eton)
Dr John Gilbert (Merchant Taylors)
Giles Radice (Winchester)
Jack Straw (Brentwood)
Mark Fisher (Eton)
Michael Foot (Leighton Park)
Harriet Harman (St Paul's Girls School)

Ten things which link the assassinations of Abraham Lincoln and John Kennedy

Lincoln was elected President in 1860; Kennedy was elected in 1960

Lincoln had a secretary called Kennedy; Kennedy had a secretary called Lincoln

The assassins, John Wilkes Booth and Lee Harvey Oswald, were both Southerners in their twenties

Both Presidents were shot in the head

Both assassinations took place on a Friday

Lincoln was shot in a theatre by a man who hid in a warehouse; Kennedy was shot from a warehouse by a man who hid in a theatre

Booth and Oswald both died before they could be tried

Lincoln was succeeded by Andrew Johnson; Kennedy by Lyndon Johnson

Andrew Johnson was born in 1808; Lyndon Johnson in 1908

Kennedy was riding in a Lincoln when he was shot

Ten reasons to vote Green

That David Icke seems a nice young man
The Monster Raving Loony Party needs some serious
    competition
You're worried about all the lead in pencils
You don't want the ice caps in your gin and tonic to melt
You're in favour of saving Wales
You work for a firm which makes roll-on deodorant
It won't affect the result
You feel guilty about the fur coat you once bought
Global warming doesn't seem to have cut down your heating
    bills
Someone has to

A handy guide to the situation in Eastern Europe

Democratisation: Even party officials have to queue for bread
Free press: Stories about Elvis sightings in Red Square
New generation of leaders: Anyone under the age of seventy
Old guard: Men in 1950s suits
Hardliner: Someone who never smiles
Reformer: Owns a pair of Levi's
Modernisation: Supermarkets with 'Five Cabbages or Less'
    checkouts
Free elections: Choice between socialism and socialism
Concessions: Lulu records available in the shops
Westernisation: Big increase in street crime

Ten politicians who have cried in public

Bob Hawke, Australian PM, admitting that he had been unfaithful to his wife

Senator Ed Muskie, when asked about his wife's drinking, during the 1972 New Hampshire primaries

Benazir Bhutto, as she cast her vote in the 1988 general election in Pakistan

Lord George-Brown, paying a tribute to John F. Kennedy after his assassination

Michael Dukakis, on the 1988 US presidential campaign trail

Gerald Ford, reading his letter of congratulation to Jimmy Carter after being defeated in the 1980 US presidential election

Alexei Kosygin, after the announcement of the death of President Nasser

Richard Nixon, during the Watergate scandal

Winston Churchill, in the House of Commons, when discussing the Blitz

Pat Schroeder, reputedly tough US Democratic Congresswoman, announcing in 1987 that she would not be running for President

Ten parliamentary candidates who didn't get elected

Pamela Stephenson

Jonathan King

Vanessa Redgrave

Eric Morley

Ludovic Kennedy

Cynthia Payne

Auberon Waugh

Robin Day

A. L. Rowse

William Douglas Home

Ten MPs' hobbies

Kenneth Baker (writing poetry)
Harry Greenway (parachuting)
Audrey Wise (rearing chickens)
Nicholas Ridley (salmon fishing)
Edwina Currie (rifle shooting)
Greville Janner (magic)
Dennis Skinner (heel-and-toe walking)
Bryan Gould (cooking)
Kenneth Clarke (bird-watching)
Ken Livingstone (collecting newts)

Tory MP-speak: a guide to interpretation

We're right behind the Prime Minister: After you with the knife

Conservatism is all about conserving things: Especially my career

Inflation is still the number one enemy: The Poll Tax is the number one enemy

The Community Charge is about local accountability: And I'm going to pay with my seat

This really isn't the time to make waves: Why can't Michael keep his mouth shut?

It's time for a return to old-style conservatism: That woman really must go

Of course we're not happy with the opinion polls: They should be banned

There's a long time until the election: We could become even more unpopular

I'm prepared to serve the Party in any capacity: Move over, Margaret

All Governments suffer from mid-term blues: Why can't we do something popular, like bring back hanging?

Ten things that might as well have been on Neville Chamberlain's 'piece of paper'

Eva Braun's telephone number
A Scrabble word worth 276 points
A secret design for waxed *Lederhosen*
Marlene Dietrich's autograph
An order for an M&S cardigan for Goering
Himmler's theories on the 4–2–4 system
Train times from Berlin to Poland
Hitler's own recipe for *Knackwürst*
A particularly difficult chess problem
Last night's greyhound results

Politicians who appeared in films

Benito Mussolini (as an extra in *The Eternal City*, USA, 1914)
Michael Foot (as himself in *Rockets Galore*, Britain, 1958)
Fidel Castro (an extra in *Holiday in Mexico*, USA, 1946)
Ed Koch (as himself in *The Muppets Take Manhattan*, USA, 1984)
Jomo Kenyatta (an African chief in *Sanders of the River*, Britain, 1935)
Leon Trotsky (bit part in *My Official Wife*, USA, 1914)
Gough Whitlam (as himself in *Barry McKenzie Holds His Own*, Australia, 1974)
Yitzhak Rabin (as himself in *Operation Thunderbolt*, Israel, 1977)
Hubert Humphrey (as himself in *The Candidate*, USA, 1972)
Theodore Roosevelt (as himself in *Womanhood, The Glory of a Nation*, USA, 1917)

Where fiction is stranger than truth – ten fictional works featuring Mrs Thatcher

God And All His Angels (novel by Graham Lord)
Titmuss Regained (novel by John Mortimer)
For Your Eyes Only (James Bond film)
First Among Equals (novel by Jeffrey Archer)
The Negotiator (novel by Frederick Forsyth)
Operation 10 (novel by Hardiman Scott)
Anyone for Denis (West End comedy)
XPD (novel by Len Deighton)
Electric Beach (novel by Laurence Rees)
The Child in Time (novel by Ian McEwan)

A selection of films for politicians

Dr Strangelove: Or How I Learned to Stop Worrying and Love the Bomb (Neil Kinnock)
The Great Dictator (Margaret Thatcher)
The Man Who Never Was (Robert Maclennan)
The Blob (Nigel Lawson)
The Incredible Shrinking Man (Colin Moynihan)
Dr No (David Owen)
Guess Who's Coming to Dinner (Roy Hattersley)
Rebel Without A Cause (Edward Heath)
And Then There Were None (Any member of the SDP)
Lord Jim (James Callaghan)

Miscellany

Ten things to chill the heart of the Queen

It's a Royal Knockout II
Peter Greenaway's latest fim is chosen for a Royal Command
    Performance
Margaret Thatcher wins the next General Election
The Duchess of York co-writes a book with Princess Michael
    of Kent
Prince Charles reveals that his plants are now answering back
Any display of traditional folk dancing on a royal tour
The Royal Variety Show goes twice-yearly
Prince Philip announces that in future he is going to say what
    he thinks
Mad corgi disease sweeps Britain
Prince Edward starts to work out at the YMCA

Just when you thought things couldn't get any worse . . .

The Samaritans hang up
You mistake the fly spray for deodorant
The England football squad releases an album
Your face appears on the front of *Sunday Sport*
The person you wake up with can't remember your name
Your new company car is a Trabant
Your passport photograph has a piece of spinach between the
    front teeth
You discover the vicar reading a copy of *Viz*
Your company relocates to Northern Ireland
You get roped into *Surprise Surprise*

Ten reasons for failing a driving test

Trying to start the car from the back seat
Failing to signal before turning into a canal
Sitting on the edge of the sun roof and steering with your feet
Balancing a Jack Russell terrier on your lap throughout the
    test
Successfully shaking off a police car
Doing an emergency stop in the middle of a roundabout
Mounting a pensioner
Dropping your cigarette between the examiner's legs
Stopping to buy a six-pack of lager without permission
Offering the examiner a nip from your hip flask to calm his
    nerves

Forget Lemsip – ten old wives' cures for the common cold

Wear two unwashed socks under your shirt collar for five days
Drink a cup of fresh barley water in which three snails have
    been boiled
Rub your teeth and throat daily with a garlic clove
Catch nine bees in a cup and allow each to sting your left
    forearm
Shave your head and smear it with a mixture of cow dung and
    maiden's water
Sleep with a sprig of mint under your pillow
Take the webs of three spiders, place in a silk purse and wear
    around your neck
Eat a whole mouse fried in batter
Soak the spleen of a goose in vinegar and drink one teaspoon
    of the liquid every hour
Toast the skin of a banana, grind to powder, mix with tobacco
    and smoke

Man's best friend: a guide to interpretation

Almost human: Lies slumped in front of the TV for hours
Friendly: Sniffs in embarrassing places
Well-trained: Feigns sleep when it's time for a walk
A man's dog: Knows the route to the pub
Lovable: Doesn't mind wearing bootees and a tartan coat
Perfect guard dog: Never stops barking
Independent: We never see it
Good with children: No teeth
Faithful: To anyone who feeds it
Playful: Digs up next door's flower beds

Ten people who take themselves too seriously

Sting
Kate Adie
Simon Bates
Martin Amis
Emma Thompson

Charles Dance
Linda McCartney
Woody Allen
Sebastian Coe
Kenneth Branagh

Can you spot a bore? Ten conversation-stoppers from their repertoire

The twenty-first century doesn't start until 2001
The Beatles were turned down by Decca Records
Humphrey Bogart never said 'Play it again, Sam'
There were only two series of *Fawlty Towers*
Horst Buchholz and Brad Dexter are the two you can never
    think of in *The Magnificent Seven*
John Major's father was a trapeze artist
There are more Jews in New York than there are in Israel
Andy Warhol said one day everybody will be famous for
    fifteen minutes
Benidorm was once a quiet fishing village
Dennis Waterman played *Just William* on TV

Strange brews: ten curiously-named local beers

Wobbly Bob (Old Mill Brewery, Humberside)
Willy Warmer (Crouch Vale Brewery, Essex)
Knightly Brew (Premier Brewery, West Midlands)
Headbanger (Archers Brewery, Wiltshire)
Old Buzzard (Cotleigh Brewery, Somerset)
Tanglefoot (Hall & Woodhouse Brewery, Dorset)
Owd Roger (Marston's Brewery, Staffordshire)
Force Nine (Whitby Brewery, North Yorkshire)
Pendle Witches Brew (Morehouses Brewery, Lancashire)
Old Peculier (Theakston's Brewery, North Yorkshire)

Ten people who achieved immortality in the dictionary – look them up any time

Maverick: Sam Maverick, Texas rancher who owned but did not brand cattle

Bloomers: Amelia Bloomer, social reformer who advocated these undergarments

Quisling: Vidkun Quisling, Norwegian collaborator with the Nazis

Dobermann: Herr L. Dobermann, German dog breeder

Guillotine: Joseph Guillotin, campaigner for 'humane' capital punishment during the French Revolution

Leotard: Jules Léotard, nineteenth-century French trapeze artist

Lynch: William Lynch, Virginian judge who dispensed rough justice

Stetson: John Stetson, Philadelphia hat maker

Hooligan: Patrick Hooligan, Irish gang leader

Nicotine: Jean Nicot, sixteenth-century French ambassador who discovered tobacco's alkaloid

Go round the world without leaving Britain

Egypt (Hampshire)
Holland (Surrey)
America (Shropshire)
Canada (Hampshire)
Moscow (Strathclyde)
California (Norfolk)
Greenland (South Yorkshire)
New England (Cambridgeshire)
Rhodesia (Nottinghamshire)
New Zealand (Derbyshire)

Ten words which have no rhymes (go on, try it)

Bilge	Orange
Bulb	Scarce
Cusp	Spoilt
Film	Twelfth
Month	Warmth

Ten unsung inventors

Margaret Knight: the flat-bottomed paper bag (1869)
Joseph Glidden: barbed wire (1874)
William Painter: the crown bottle cap (1892)
Horace Short: the loudspeaker (1900)
John C. Dunton: the jukebox (1905)
Jacques Brandenberger: cellophane (1908)
Georges Claude: neon light (1910)
Sylvan Goldman: the shopping trolley (1937)
Chester Carlson: the photocopier (1938)
Peter Goldmark: the LP record (1948)

Meet the county set

Susan Hampshire
David Essex
Ann Clywd
Bruce Kent
Carole Cleveland

Leonard Cheshire
Judith Durham
Devon Malcolm
Somerset Maugham
Ray Dorset

Oops! Ten people who read their own (premature) obituaries

Harold Macmillan
Max Jaffa
Alfred Nobel
Mark Twain
Max Robertson
Wild Bill Hickok
Lynne Carol (*Coronation Street*'s Martha Longhurst)
Bertrand Russell
Daniel Boone
P. T. Barnum

Ten aliases used by royals

Charlie Chester (Prince Charles)
Mrs Smith (Princess Diana)
Mr and Mrs Hardy (Prince and Princess of Wales)
The Countess of Leicester (The Queen)
Mrs Green (Duchess of Kent)
Norman Gordon (Lord Snowdon)
Edward Bishop (Prince Edward)
Mrs Brown (Princess Margaret)
Mr Kent (Angus Ogilvy)
Andrew Cambridge (Prince Andrew)

Ten people on a map of Britain

Annbank (Strathclyde)
Bettyhill (Highlands)
Marygold (Borders)
Charlesworth (Derbyshire)
Ericstane (Dumfries)

Georgeham (Devon)
Ivychurch (Kent)
Mablethorpe (Lincolnshire)
Oswaldtwistle (Lancashire)
Peterlee (Durham)

Are you cut out to be a polytechnic lecturer? Ten tell-tale signs

You own a paisley kipper tie
Your 2CV is festooned with ecologically significant stickers
You listen to Emerson, Lake and Palmer
You make your own wine
You read modern poets
Your favourite word is 'bourgeois'
You own too many LPs to contemplate buying a CD player
You haven't thrown away your loons
You voted Green in the Euro-elections
You lament the passing of the *Old Grey Whistle Test*

Ten names which lose something in the translation

Giovanni Casanova: John Newhouse
Giuseppe Verdi: Joe Green
Henri Rousseau: Henry Redhead
Josef Stalin: Joe Steel
Julio Iglesias: Julian Church
Albert Einstein: Bert Onestone
Claudio Monteverdi: Claude Greenhill
Kurt Waldheim: Kurt Treehouse
Jean Racine: John Root
Helmut Kohl: Helmut Cabbage

'Sorry for the delay . . . ' Ten BR excuses for late trains

A lunatic climbing over a fence near the station
A rat biting through a power cable
A horse on the line
The guard left behind by accident
Ammonia from an ice rink leaking on to the line
Slippery rails
Pigs on the line at Hamstreet
Passengers fighting
A man with an umbrella on the line
High tides at Portsmouth Harbour

Ten updated Old Masters

Frans Hals: They're Laughing at My Cavalier
John Everett Millais: The Toyboyhood of Raleigh
Leonardo da Vinci: Adoration of the Maggie
William Frederick Yeames: And When Did You Last See Your
    Lager?
Sandro Botticelli: The Natural Birth of Venus
Thomas Gainsborough: The Blue Boy George
J. M. W. Turner: Rain, Steam and Signal Failure – The Great
    Network SouthEast
Leonardo da Vinci: The Last TV Supper
Sandro Botticelli: Madonna and Child (Sean Penn)
Leonardo da Vinci: The Moaning Leaseholder

Ten odd-sounding jobs

Belly builder (assembles and fits the insides of pianos)
Mother repairer (refurbishes master plates in the record
    industry)
Slubber doffer (takes bobbins of yarn from spindles in mills)
Dukey rider (guard's assistant who couples and uncouples
    carriages)
Dope sprayer (applies tanning varnish to leather hides)
Top screw (foreman of a cattle ranch)
Hooker inspector (checks cloth in a textile mill)
Necker (feeds cardboard into a box-making machine)
Foot straightener (assembles watch and clock dials)
Legend maker (arranges letters and logos to make signs)

A gourmet tour of the British Isles

Ham (Wiltshire)
Tongue (Highlands)
Sandwich (Kent)
Curry (Sligo)
Beer (Devon)

Booze (North Yorkshire)
Leek (Staffordshire)
Rye (Sussex)
Bacon End (Essex)
Great Fryup (North Yorkshire)

Ten topics of conversation to avoid when stuck in a lift

The law of gravity
The trouble last night's curry is giving you
Towering Inferno
The highly contagious bug you've picked up
Hancock's Half Hour
Random knife attacks
The Black Hole of Calcutta
Claustrophobia
Jeffrey Archer's new play
The benefits of double glazing

Ten things which have overstayed their welcome

Coffee commercials
Garfield toys stuck on car windows
Dame Edna Everage
Nostalgia for the 1960s
Privatisation
Chat shows
Books about spies in MI6
Health experts
Benefit concerts
Surrealistic ads for cigarettes

Tooth and claw – a guide to wildlife programmes

'Secrets of the deep': Hideous-faced fish that give you the willies
'Miracle of nature': Close-up shots of birth, death or mating
'Feeds on berries': No need to send the children to bed
'Moment of birth': Usually in the middle of the family supper
'Natural order of things': Something big eating something small
'Female of the species': The dun-coloured one
'Almost human': Monkeys picking their noses
'Nature's solution': Vultures clear up
'Involved months of patient filming': Cost a fortune
'This time the antelope escapes': Too distressing to show what eventually happened.

'Don't you know there's a War on?' Ten ads from World War II

On Active Service: Constipon Laxatives!
Weetabix: Your Every-Occasion Food in this Time of
    Emergency
When it's 'No Smoking' by Order Rowntrees Fruit Gums
    Refresh and Soothe
War Secret of ARP Police: 'Litesome' Bracing Underwear
For a Home Win . . . There's Nothing like Bird's Custard
Worth Knitting For: Always Use Miladi Knitting Wools
Fry's Sandwich Chocolate – The Perfect Emergency Ration
Protect Yourself in the Blackout with the New Illuminated
    Safety Flowers
Don't Take Your 'Leave' Without Bovril
Keep Smiling on 'The Home Front': Nightly Bile Beans Keep
    Up Your Health And Spirits!

'I'm not a prude, but . . .' Ten phrases that land with a deafening thud

'I don't mind people having a good time, but . . .'
'I've always considered myself broadminded, but . . .'
'I don't really see what the point is . . .'
'I appreciate a joke as much as the next person, but . . .'
'I've no wish to spoil anyone's enjoyment, but . . .'
'I think of myself as a typical viewer, but . . .'
'I'm more concerned about the effect it could have on others . . .'
'I was young myself once, but . . .'
'I'm not one of life's complainers, but . . .'
'I'm all for artistic licence, but . . .'

Ten cherished Goon Show titles

Insurance – The White Man's Burden
I Was Monty's Treble
The Collapse of the British Railway Sandwich System
Drums Along the Mersey
The Affair of the Lone Banana
The String Robberies
I Knew Terence Nuke
The Dreaded Batter Pudding Hurler (of Bexhill-on-Sea)
The Chinese Legs
Crime Does Not Pay Income Tax

And you think the Poll Tax is bad – ten earlier English taxes

Beard tax (1558)
Hearth tax (1662)
Chimney tax (1691)
Window tax (1696)
Male servants tax (1777)
Female servants tax (1793)
Dog tax (1793)
Clock tax (1793)
Hair powder tax (1793)
Bread tax (1815)

A world map of people

Mike England
Kathy Jordan
Jools Holland
Nancy Spain
Alan Brazil

Jill Ireland
Ken Scotland
Pierre Mendès-France
India Hicks
Josey Wales

'I've started, but somebody else can finish' – ten unfinished works completed by others

Raymond Chandler's *Poodle Springs*, completed by Robert B. Parker

Robert Louis Stevenson's *St Ives*, completed by Sir Arthur Quiller-Couch, and also Jenni Calder

Puccini's *Turandot*, completed by Franco Alfano

Charles Dickens' *The Mystery of Edwin Drood*, completed by Leon Garfield

Mozart's *Requiem*, completed by Franz Sussmayer

Mahler's Tenth Symphony, completed by Deryck Cooke

Arthur Sullivan's *The Emerald Isle*, completed by Edward German

Mussorgsky's *Khovanshchina*, orchestrated and completed by Rimsky-Korsakov

J. M. Barrie's *Shall We Join The Ladies*, completed by L. E. Jones

Beethoven's 'Tenth' Symphony, completed by Dr Barry Cooper

Everybody's doing it – ten people who should launch their own perfumes

Eau d'Excess (Julian Clary)
Indulgence (Roy Hattersley)
Shameless (The Duchess of York)
Forever Me (Margaret Thatcher)
Intemperance (John McEnroe)
Extravagance (Imelda Marcos)
Inexplicable (Dennis Potter)
Connections (Pamella Bordes)
Ever Hopeful (Michael Heseltine)
Essence de Possum (Dame Edna Everidge)

Doctor-speak: a guide to interpretation

I'm afraid I've got some bad news: My golf match on Saturday
    has been cancelled

This won't hurt at all: This won't hurt me at all

Call me Steve: Don't you just love *St Elsewhere*?

Do you have an appointment?: You really must plan ahead if
    you're going to be ill

I want you to try some of these: I'll be fascinated to know if
    they work

There's certainly something to be said for alternative
    medicine: But not by me there isn't

Stick your tongue out and say 'Aah': I'm fully qualified, you
    know

Private practice isn't for me: I'm perfectly happy with my
    black BMW

I can refer you to a consultant if you wish: How dare you
    question my competence?

Of course, I may be wrong: This man is not a doctor

Ten people you'll never forget

Your driving instructor
The person who was always top of the class
The prisoner when you were on jury service
Your first boss
The teacher you hated
The teacher you loved
Your first serious love
The school bully
The nurse who looked after you
The couple who never returned your dinner invitation

Ten specialist subjects for Mastermind contestants

The life and works of Magnus Magnusson
The music of Zager and Evans
The avocado bathroom suite: its place in English interior
    design
House prices 1980 to 1990
The role of humour in the works of Leonard Cohen
Victorian architecture in Milton Keynes
The novels of Ben Elton
The commercials of Griff Rhys Jones 1985 to 1990
The life and perks of ex-Tory Cabinet Ministers
Journolists

The animal kingdom – ten beastly place names

Badger, Shropshire
Dog Village, Devon
Horse Island, Strathclyde
Donkey Town, Surrey
Sheep Hill, Tyne and Wear

Swallow, Lincolnshire
Frog End, Cambridgeshire
Toad Row, Suffolk
Tadpole Bridge, Oxfordshire
Monkey Island, Berkshire

'And one luxury item . . .' Ten pointless things to ask for on Desert Island Discs

Any game for 'two players or more'
A chatline directory
A wall-mounted can opener
A Tupperware catalogue
A Christmas cracker
Your credit cards
A supply of self-adhesive post-it notes
A set of saloon-style louvred doors
An ashtray
A knitted doll loo-roll cover

Ten people who should have won a Nobel Prize

Graham Greene
Thomas Edison
J. K. Galbraith
Patrick Steptoe
Bob Geldof

Jonas Salk
H. G. Wells
Sigmund Freud
Joseph Lister
P. G. Wodehouse

Ten men whose names make as much sense backwards

Kirk Douglas
Ray Charles
Barry Norman
Clive James
Paul Nicholas

Leslie Thomas
Elton John
Andrew Neil
George Michael
Nicholas Ray

Ten more challenges for Anneka

Resurrect the SDP
Repair the ozone layer
Take Britain into the European Monetary System
Remake *Gone with the Wind*
Launch a Sunday newspaper
Stop grinning for two minutes
Write a book of lists
Design a skyscraper that Prince Charles likes
Find Lord Lucan
Raise the *Titanic*

Ten things to be brave about

Pogonophobia (fear of beards)
Hyalinopygophobia (fear of glass bottoms)
Genuphobia (fear of knees)
Acarophobia (fear of itching)
Thaasophobia (fear of sitting idle)
Iophobia (fear of rust)
Aulophobia (fear of flutes)
Chrometophobia (fear of money)
Dikephobia (fear of justice)
Keraunothnetophobia (fear of falling man-made satellites)

Ten things which aren't what they seem

The funny-bone is not a bone; it's a nerve
A glow-worm is not a worm; it's a beetle
Bombay duck is not a duck; it's dried fish
Great Danes do not come from Denmark; they originated in
    Germany
Lead pencils contain no lead; they contain graphite
Chop suey is not a Chinese dish; it's American
A silkworm is not a worm; it's a caterpillar
A sea anemone is not a plant; it's an animal
A shooting star is not a star; it's a meteor
Sweetbread is not bread; it is the pancreas or thymus gland of
    an animal

Baby-talk: a guide to interpretation

Takes after his father: Snores and suffers from wind
No trouble at all: We have a nanny
Advanced for his age: Likes a drop of gin in his milk
Already interested in books: Sucks them
Sense of humour: Makes rude noises when we've got
    company
Lovable: Fat
Creative: Likes to put his dinner on his head
A real little boy: Assaults his sister
A real little girl: Always having tantrums
An April baby: Never dry

Are you sitting comfortably? Ten facts to make you squirm

Of the 12,000 snakes used in *Raiders of the Lost Ark*, around 2000 went missing

An estimated 40,000 people die from snake bites each year, 75 per cent of them in India

A bowl of highly-prized rat snake soup can cost up to £80 in Hong Kong

In the 1930s a Burmese jewellery salesman was swallowed feet first by a python

The most poisonous snake is the sea snake, whose venom is one hundred times more potent than that of any other snake

A snake's headless body once continued writhing for 2½ days after decapitation

The largest animal known to have been swallowed by a snake was a 130-pound impala, found in an African rock python

It is illegal to eat snake in Iraq on a Sunday

More people die from snake bites in Burma than from traffic accidents

Snake gall bladder, considered an aphrodisiac, can fetch £5000 a pound in Asia

Ten acronyms which try too hard

CISSY (Campaign to Impede Sex Stereotyping in the Young)
LAGER (Liberal Action Group for Electoral Reform)
HOWL (Hands off Wildlife)
RAPE (Richmond Association for the Preservation of the
    Environment)
CALM (Campaign Against the Lorry Menace)
MUSTARD (Multiracial Union of Squatters to Alleviate
    Racial Discrimination)
FACTS (Football Association Coaching Tactics Skills)
SENSE (Society for Ending Needless and Silly Expenditure)
ALAS (Association of the Chartered Land Agents' Society)
STRIVE (Society for the Preservation of Rural Industries and
    Village Enterprises)

Selling God – ten posters seen outside churches

Fight truth decay – brush up your Bible every day
Come in for a faith lift
Seven prayer-less days make one spiritually weak
The Good Book has more chapters than the bad box has
    channels
Come to Ch**ch. What is missing?
It's impossible to lose your footing on your knees
Sing a hymn for Him
Jog to church and keep spiritually fit
Bank on God for a higher rate of interest
Danger! Live Church!

Ten things beauty contestants want to be . . . and what they'd settle for

Explorer (a tour operator's representative)
TV presenter (a TV game show hostess)
A professional sportswoman (receptionist in a health club)
Top model (a two-page spread in *Mayfair*)
Architect (promotional work for Wimpey)
Mother Teresa (a £5 donation to Oxfam)
International businesswoman (interviewing people for life
        insurance policies)
Prime Minister (a supporting role in a political sex scandal)
A doctor (a Cambridge Diet counsellor)
Miss World (marriage to a TV personality)

Ten more ads from World War II

Going Bald? Silvikrin Does Grow Hair
Tuck in the Tummy: Little Corporal Reducing Belt and
        Supporting Shorts Combined!
Bargains by Post: Genuine London Busmen's Trousers, 5/9d
Simpson Iodine Socks: With Reinforced Iodine!
Nice People with Nice Manners Use Talc after their Bath:
        Coty Talc for Freshness Appeal
White Horse Whisky: This is what you Need for a Long,
        Sound Sleep
Dentesive: Stops False Teeth Click
New Life for Every Man! Huttons Brand Gland Tablets
New Feet! Omniped Elastic Foot Cushion from International
        Foot Appliances, 3/11d
To Maintain Youthful Fitness Men in their Prime Take
        Beecham's Pills

A top ten of villages

Onehouse (Suffolk)
Two Bridges (Glos.)
Three Chimneys (Kent)
Four Forks (Somerset)
Five Oak Green (Kent)

Six Mile Bottom (Cambs.)
Seven Sisters (Glamorgan)
Eight Ash Green (Essex)
Nine Elms (Wiltshire)
Ten Mile Bank (Norfolk)

Ten worthless accolades

Pipesmoker of the year
The best-dressed MP in the House of Commons
England's most promising fast bowler
The cleverest man of his generation
The most outstanding performance in a Royal Variety Show
Colchester United's player of the season
Tie wearer of the year
ITV's most popular sitcom
Best foreign language film at any festival
Tastiest low-alcohol lager

Ten items which always turn up at jumble sales

A flask without a top
A 1972 *Judy Annual*
The insides of a television set
A pair of nearly new platform shoes
A lamp base decorated with glazed pebbles
An LP by Kenny Ball and his Jazzmen
A model aircraft with the undercarriage missing
A 1000-piece jigsaw
A Worthington 'E' ashtray
A paraffin heater which needs some attention

Ten theories that never got off the ground

Illness can be cured by shining different coloured lights on
the afflicted parts of the body (Col Dinshah Ghadiali,
1920)

Education can cause a woman's uterus to shrivel (Dr E.
Clarke, 1873)

Thinking is done by tiny creatures in the brain called menorgs
and disorgs (Alfred Lawson, early twentieth century)

The deceased should be preserved by electroplating them (Dr
Varlot, 1891)

The earth is a hollow shell and we live on the inside (Cyrus
Reed Teed, 1870)

Men and women are two different species, descended from
different animals (William Smyth, 1927)

Women who want to give birth to girls should eat a high
protein diet, and avoid eggs, fish, meat and cheese if
they want boys (Dr Israel Bram, 1914)

The sun is a lens made of ice which creates heat by focusing
the brilliance of God (Charles Palmer, 1878)

Wheat was given to us by extra-terrestrials called the Manu
(W. Scott-Elliot, 1896)

The weight of moonlight on the oceans causes the water to
spread out to the edges of the land (G. E. Last,
nineteenth century)

'Cave, chaps, it's Smuggins!' Ten school nicknames

Prince Edward: Jaws
Michael Caine: The Professor
Warren Beatty: Little Henry
Sybil Ruscoe: Scribble
Beryl Bainbridge: Basher

Bob Geldof: Liver lips
Grace Jones: Firefly
Prince Philip: Flop
Twiggy: Sticks
Nigel Lawson: Smuggins

The case for the defence: a guide to interpretation

My comments will be brief: There is no defence

My client intends that this will not happen again: He intends
not to get caught again

If you find the defendant guilty, then you find society guilty:
I've been watching *LA Law*

I don't want to waste the court's time: I don't want to waste
my time

Now we come to the matter of the sawn-off shotgun: You
aren't going to believe this

In no way do I wish to minimise the gravity of the offence:
Why do I always get shoplifting cases?

Is illegal use of a hosepipe so serious?: It is when it's used to
beat someone over the head

He will have to live with this for the rest of his life: Come on,
he's only charged with having no MoT certificate

I submit there is no case to answer: I submit

We intend to appeal: Why not? There could be a miracle

Ten proverbs which are patently untrue

The best things in life are free
Barking dogs seldom bite
You can't judge a book by its cover
Life begins at forty
It never rains but it pours
An apple a day keeps the doctor away
Ask no questions and you'll hear no lies
You can't teach an old dog new tricks
Every cloud has a silver lining
He who laughs last laughs loudest

Ten explanations for the mystery of the Marie Celeste

The ship was manned by lemmings
The tour company went bust
Beadle was about
The captain had insisted on another charades evening
It was an elaborate PR stunt for the *Goon Show*'s 'Mystery of
       the Marie Celeste (Solved)', broadcast in 1954
It was a Taste of Euthanasia cruise
The cabaret starred Jim Bowen
Everyone is trapped in a future episode of *Star Trek*
Sue Lawley gave them all eight records and told them to find
       a desert island
They'd heard about the Poll Tax

Ten new words for the dictionary

Beadle *v*. To giggle uncontrollably at human misery and
       embarrassment
Billoddie *n*. Unconvincing enthusiasm
Cilla *n*. Point at which everyone tries to switch channels
Cleese *n*. That part of a man's leg visible between the sock
       and trouser hem
Lloydwebba *n*. Musical term for the sound made by a box-
       office cash register
Gower *v*. To maintain an air of nonchalance in the face of
       adversity
Minogue *n*. High-pitched sound audible only to girls between
       the ages of eight and thirteen
Rushton *n*. End panellist on a TV quiz game
Stalloni *n*. Bicep-shaped pasta shells
Tarbuck *n*. A joke which has had several previous owners

And finally . . . Start with an earthquake and build up to a climax – opening lines that make you want to read on:

'As Gregor Samsa awoke one morning from uneasy dreams he found himself transformed in his bed into a gigantic insect' (Franz Kafka, *Metamorphosis*)

If you want to know the other nine, you'll have to wait for the next YOU Magazine *Book of Journolists*, coming to a bookshop near you next year!